ESSENTIAL LIFE SKILLS SERIES

WHAT YOU NEED TO KNOW ABOUT

READING SIGNS, DIRECTORIES, SCHEDULES, MAPS, CHARTS & UTILITY BILLS

Second Edition

Carolyn Morton Starkey   Norgina Wright Penn

National Textbook Company
a division of NTC *Publishing Group* • Lincolnwood, Illinois USA

ACKNOWLEDGMENTS

American Automobile Association, map. Copyright © AAA.
Appalachian Power Co., bill
Bluefield Gas Co., bill
General Drafting Co., Inc., maps. Copyright © General Drafting Co.,
   Inc. All rights reserved.
Hammond, Inc., map. Reprinted from *Hammond Road Atlas and
   Vacation Guide.* Copyright © Hammond, Inc.
Michigan Bell Telephone Co., telephone materials
Mid-Manhattan Library of New York, floor plan

Preface

This revised edition from the Essential Life Skills Series tells you what you need to know about reading directories, signs, maps, schedules, and utility bills. Mastering these reading skills will make you more assertive and self-confident. You will learn to cope better with everyday situations.

This book covers some familiar yet very important materials. You will learn to read and understand:

floor plans	maps
building directories	schedules
telephone books	charts
street and highway signs	bills

Throughout the book you will find examples of real signs, maps, schedules, charts, and bills, like the ones you see and use every day.

Each section in this book includes definitions of words that may be new or difficult. Checkup sections help you review what you have learned. There are many opportunities to practice your skills.

Because of its flexible format, this book can be used either for self-study or in a group setting with an instructor. The answer key is on perforated pages so that it is easy to remove.

When you have mastered the skills in this book, you will want to develop other skills to become more successful in our modern world. The other books in the Essential Life Skills Series will show you how.

Essential Life Skills Series

What You Need to Know about Reading Labels, Directions & Newspapers 5655-2

What You Need to Know about Reading Ads, Reference Materials & Legal Documents 5656-0

What You Need to Know about Getting a Job and Filling Out Forms 5657-9

What You Need to Know about Reading Signs, Directories, Schedules, Maps, Charts & Utility Bills 5658-7

What You Need to Know about Basic Writing Skills, Letters & Consumer Complaints 5659-6

Contents

Using Directories

Special Reading Skills

Using directories

When you look up numbers in a telephone book, you use a directory. When you read a list of departments in a store, you use a directory. A shopping mall or library may display floor plans with directories. These help you find locations or information fast. Directories can save you time.

In this section, you will practice using directories and floor plans.

Directories and floor plans

> **WORDS TO KNOW**
>
> **annex**   an addition to a building
>
> **directory**   a listing of names and addresses
>
> **floor plan**   a drawing showing the size and arrangement of rooms on each floor of a building
>
> **mezzanine**   a low story between two main stories in a building, usually above the ground floor, sometimes in the form of a balcony

Directories are alphabetical listings. They are in book form like the telephone book. They are in display form like those in department stores. They help you find an address or a phone number. They help you find which floor an office is on. They help you locate what you want in a big store. Directories are arranged in several different ways.

Some directories are simply alphabetical lists. The white pages of the telephone book is one such alphabetical list. In the white pages you can find telephone numbers listed by a person's last name. You can also find business listings under the name of the business.

Some directories are arranged by headings. Headings in the yellow pages of the telephone book are alphabetized. For example, AUTOMOBILES are listed before RESTAURANTS in the yellow pages. Entries under the headings are then alphabetized.

Another way to arrange a directory is to list the floors of a store or office building in order, then to list items by their floor location. Another way is to use section headings such as the sections of a shopping mall.

A floor plan is both a map and a directory. With a floor plan you get both a list of items *and* a drawing. Floor plans can be very helpful for buildings with a number of stores, for example, shopping malls.

Activity 1
Using store directories

Department store directories are usually arranged like the directory below. Use this directory of Morton's Bargain City to locate the items listed below. On which floor would you find each of these items?

Morton's Bargain City

	Floor		Floor
Appliances	1	Infants' Wear	3
Books	2	Lingerie	2
Cafeteria	2	Luggage	1
Children's Wear	3	Men's Wear	2
Cosmetics	2	Office Supplies	1
Domestics	3	Shoes	2
Handbags	2	Toys	1
Infants' Furniture	3	Women's Wear	2

---

1. Baby Crib _____

2. Baby Doll _____

3. Make-up _____

4. Ladies' Dresses _____

5. Man's Shirt _____

6. Boots _____

7. Dishwasher _____

8. Index Cards _____

9. Purse _____

10. Baby Blanket _____

11. Lunch _____

12. Cookware _____

13. Novel _____

14. Hosiery _____

15. Bicycle _____

16. Clothes Dryer _____

17. Typewriter _____

18. Ladies' Pants _____

19. Linen _____

20. Stroller _____

21. Refrigerator _____

22. Bath Towels _____

23. Nightgown _____

24. File Folders _____

25. Coffee Maker _____

26. Sneakers _____

27. Briefcase _____

28. Hair Dryer _____

29. Man's Tie _____

30. Baseball Bat _____

Activity 2

Using a floor directory for a department store

This is a floor directory. A floor directory is often found on or near the elevators of large department stores. It lists each floor. It also lists what may be found on each floor. Use the sample floor directory to answer the questions below.

MAIN FLOOR

Girl's Wear
Women's Wear

SECOND FLOOR

Accessories
Boy's Wear
Budget Dresses
Ladies' Lounge

THIRD FLOOR

Alterations
Coats
Men's Wear
Men's Lounge

FOURTH FLOOR

Furniture
Carpeting

FIFTH FLOOR

Housewares
Silverware

SIXTH FLOOR

Hair Salons
Pillows, Linen, Bedding

SEVENTH FLOOR

Personnel Office/Credit
Rest Rooms

On which floor would you get off the elevator if . . . .

1. you wanted to pay on your charge account?_____

2. you wanted to price a microwave oven?_____

3. you were on the fifth floor and you wanted to go to the nearest rest room?_____

4. you were Jennifer Mallory and you wanted to pick up your husband's suit?_____

5. you were Tom Mallory and you promised to meet Jennifer on the carpet floor?_____

6. you were looking for a small appliance to give as a wedding gift?_____

7. you had a hair appointment at the store's "Sophisticated Scissors" hair salon?_____

8. you were looking for furniture for your new apartment?_____

9. you wanted to apply for a job as a salesperson?_____

10. you wanted to report an error on your bill?_____

3

Activity 3
Using building directories

This is the building directory for The Enterprise Tower. It lists all offices in the building. Use this directory to answer the questions below:

Building Directory

	Floor		Floor
Acme Enterprises	10	Kilpatrick Construction	8
Armstrong Gallery	10	Kroop Advertising	2
Bear & Bear Job Consultants	8	LeGrand, J. S., M.D.	6
Barclay Consultants	10	Lerner, Paul, M.D.	6
Bartlett & Bartlett Law Offices	10	Longman Employment	3
Boston, Harry E., D.D.S.	7	Martin Wholesalers	8
Brown, Boveri, & Barton Corp.	10	Martin, W. E., M.D.	6
C&H Associates	2	Marvel Photos	4
Carteret Bank	3	Mondi Exports	8
Christens, Herman, M.D.	6	Morrison, Paul, D.D.S.	7
Claytor, Harold, M.D.	6	Neal & Neal Consultants	2
Cutler, Stanley, Attorney	5	Neptune Unlimited	3
Cyrus, Walter, Attorney	5	Nile Products	10
D'Angelo, Kenneth, M.D.	6	O'Shea, Matthew, M.D.	6
Daniels, David, M.D.	6	Rosenberg Studios	2
Daniels Realty	2	Sanchez, Carlos, D.D.S.	7
Designer Fur Headquarters	3	Sanchez, Louis, D.D.S.	7
Family Health Center	6	Santiago, Louis, M.D.	6
Flynn & Flynn Accounting Firm	4	Sibeski Brothers	5
Ferrell Employment Agency	4	Tami Studios	5
Goldman, Ronald, M.D.	6	Technical Labs	2
Green, Terry Phillip, M.D.	6	Tutor Computers	2
Green, Thomas, M.D.	7	Tutor Electronics	2
Higgins, Higgins, & Higgins	8	Tyler Textiles	8
Ingram Consultants	9	Wong's Distributors	10
International Banking Inc.	10	World Enterprises	10
International Publishing	10	World Health Inc.	6
J&E Imports	10	World Publishers	8
J&W Exports	10	Young Galleries	2
Jones & Jones Enterprises	9	Zee, Pauline, M.D.	6

1. On which floor will you find J&E Imports?_____

   J&W Exports?_____

2. On which floor will you find the legal offices of Bartlett & Barlett?_____

3. Does Dr. Harold Green have an office in this building?_____

4. Does Dr. Ronald Goldman have an office in this building?_____

5. On which floor is Wong's Distributors?_____

6. Is Kroop Advertising located in this building?_____

7. What listing comes *before* Dr. W. E. Martin's name?_____

8. What listing comes after Dr. Martin's name?_____

9. If this directory is on the first floor, how many floors will you have to walk up in order to visit the Young Galleries?_____

10. If you were on the 5th floor and used the elevator to go to Dr. Terry Green's office, how many floors up would you travel?_____

11. On what floor is Dr. Green?_____

12. The first number of the office numbers in the Tower stands for the "floor." Complete the *Room Numbers* of these offices:

Dr. Harry Boston	____08
Sibeski Brothers	____02
Dr. Harold Claytor	____11
Dr. David Daniels	____13
Dr. Paul Morrison	____07
Dr. Pauline Zee	____05
World Enterprises	____13
Tami Studios	____10

Using floor plans

Using a floor plan is like using a map. Floor plans help you find your way. They help you in malls, shopping plazas, parks, and office buildings. The key to reading a floor plan is knowing where you are.

You must find your location on the floor plan. Then you can locate other places. Decide if your destination is in front or in back of you. Decide if it is to your left or right. See if it has a name or number. See if there is a pattern to the floor plan. Is it an L-shape? Is it a circle? Is it in sections? Are there section numbers?

Activity 4

Study the floor plan of this library.

Using floor plans

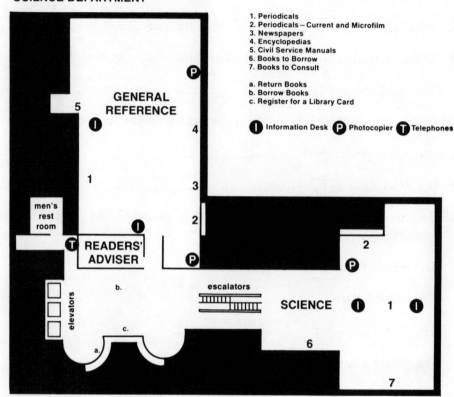

4th Floor—8 East 40th Street

GENERAL REFERENCE SERVICE
SCIENCE DEPARTMENT

1. Periodicals
2. Periodicals – Current and Microfilm
3. Newspapers
4. Encyclopedias
5. Civil Service Manuals
6. Books to Borrow
7. Books to Consult

a. Return Books
b. Borrow Books
c. Register for a Library Card

I Information Desk   **P** Photocopier   **T** Telephones

GENERAL REFERENCE

READERS' ADVISER

men's rest room

elevators

escalators

SCIENCE

Answer these questions about the fourth floor.

1. If you walk directly to the encyclopedia section from the Readers' Adviser, list the other sections you'll pass._____

_____

2. How many photocopiers are on the 4th floor?_____

3. What are the two departments on the 4th floor?_____

4. How many information desks are in each department?_____

5. Near which department is the men's rest room?_____

6. Is it possible to register for a library card on this floor?_____

CHECK YOUR UNDERSTANDING OF DIRECTORIES

Look at the following directory. It lists the stores in the Town & Country shopping mall. It also tells where on the floor plan you will find these shops. Use the directory to answer the questions.

Town & Country Shopping Mall

Allen Patton's Pets A-5
Alright Bakery B-6
Avenue Fashions D-2
Bambi Burgers C-5
Beauties Unlimited B-2
Burgers Deluxe D-3
Carolyn's Dress Boutique D-6
Charles's Chop House E-1
Chinese Cuisine A-4
Daisy's Donut Shop B-2
Dallas Kids C-1
Dandy Discount Store C-3
Deli Delight E-3
Eaton's Department Store E-9

Everybody's Place E-2
Fashions by Tanisha A-1
Gerry Grady Boutique E-4
Handsome Men's Shop B-4
House of Fashions D-5
Images Unlimited D-1
Inside Track E-5
Jazz Now E-10
Jim's Jewelries D-9
Kelly's Record Shop A-7
Kid's World E-6
Martin's Travel Agency D-8
Marci's Counter D-10
Niffy Jiffy D-7

Norge's Portraits E-8
Northwest Dance School C-4
Photographs, Inc. A-6
Plus Palace D-12
Quick Stop Mini Mart E-7
Ruth's Whichcraft B-5
Salad Bar C-2
Super Shop B-7
Tours By Toni D-4
Vicky's Hat Rack D-4
Walton's Department Store B-1
Wigs à la Nikki A-3
Your Place A-2

1. The sections of the mall are identified by letters. How many sections are there?_____

2. The mall directory lists the stores in alphabetical order. Allen Patton's Pets is the first store listed.

In which section is it found?_____

3. In which section is the House of Fashions?_____

4. You shopped at Ruth's Whichcraft, Plus Palace, and Dandy Discount Store. You had dinner at

Charles's Chop House. What is the only section you did not stop in?_____

5. You are shopping for a baby gift. List the names of two stores you might check._____

_____

7

The telephone book

Knowing how to find information in the phone book is a useful everyday skill. There are many times when you need to use the phone book. You may need to find a name, an address, or a telephone number. The telephone book has two sections. They are the white pages and the yellow pages. In larger cities, the white pages and yellow pages are separate directories.

Locating telephone numbers in the white pages

Most people are familiar with the white pages of the phone book. This is where you find the telephone numbers of people you want to call. Businesses also list their numbers in this section. But the white pages are mainly for home listings.

The white pages are easy to use if you understand how they are arranged.

Fernandez - Filbert

Fernandez, Lola 141 State St	555-8332
Fernandez, M. 4245 Burt Rd.	555-7899
Fernandez, M.L. 223 Orange Bl	555-8254
Fernandez, Martino	
8610 Gladstone Av Bloomfield	555-4149
Filbert, Abbott 61 N Park Pl	555-7083
Filbert, Alvin 2109 2nd Av	555-3321
Filbert, Bertha 18 Lane Dr	555-2578
FILBERT TOOL & DIE CO	
44 Main Lane	555-8866
Filbert, Stanley 621 Cherry St	555-5461

1. The white page listings are arranged in alphabetical order with last names first.
2. Businesses appear in the same alphabetical listings.
3. Each white page listing consists of a name, address, and telephone number.
4. Addresses will often be abbreviated. (For example, ''N'' for north, ''Rd'' for Road, ''Pk'' for Park.)
5. Headings are at the top of the white pages. They tell you the first and last names on a page.

Activity 5

Reading the white pages

Use the white page listings above to answer these questions.

1. What is the number for Lola Fernandez?_____

2. What is the number for Martino Fernandez?_____

3. What is the number for Filbert Tool & Die Co.?_____

4. What number do you call to reach Alvin Filbert on 2nd Ave.?_____

5. What number do you call to reach M. Fernandez at 4245 Burt Rd.?_____

6. What is the number for M. L. Fernandez on Orange Blvd.?_____

Activity 6

Locating telephone numbers for persons with the same names

Sometimes white page listings are confusing. Names may be similar or even the same. Answer the questions about the telephone listings below.

Jones - Jones

Jones Della 1676 Grassylawn Drive 555-8421	Jones E S 2001 Main St 555-6666
Jones Dwight 8989 Rhine Rd 555-2813	Jones Earl, MD 923 Derby Lane..................555-3245
Jones E 171 Lois Lane...............................555-8210	Jones Earl 44 Pine St Ferry Pk....................555-7110
Jones E 6 S. Ohio Ave 555-9828	Jones Earl 18095 Steel St 555-7808
Jones E 712 Colorado Blvd Farmington........555-7241	Jones Earlie 1409 Raleigh St.......................555-4648
Jones E 7918 St. Agnes..............................555-6471	Jones F 106 Wyoming Blvd 555-5523
Jones E A 817 Marked Dr 555-8010	Jones F 614 Greenlawn Ave 555-6010
Jones E C 230 Van Born Rd 555-3331	Jones Fred 601 Wright Pl............................555-7041

1. What number do you call to reach Dwight Jones?_____

2. If you are trying to reach Dr. Earl Jones, what number do you call?_____

3. What number do you dial if you are trying to reach Elizabeth Jones at 7918 St. Agnes?_____

4. How many Earl Joneses are shown?_____

5. What is the number for the Earl Jones in Ferry Park?_____

6. What number do you dial to reach E. C. Jones on Van Born Rd.?_____

The yellow pages

The yellow pages of your phone book list the names, addresses, and phone numbers of businesses. Businesses are listed under headings. Each heading will be a *service*, *product*, or *specialty*. Examples are BANKS, OFFICE SUPPLIES, and RESTAURANTS. The headings are listed alphabetically. The businesses under these headings are also listed alphabetically.

Doctors, lawyers, and dentists are also found in the yellow pages. But there are no residential listings. Businesses appear in both the white pages and the yellow pages. But the yellow pages give more information about the services they provide.

The yellow pages are a handy reference. Look at the yellow page sample on page 245. To use the yellow pages, you need to understand how they are arranged.

1. Business are listed under the service, product, or specialty they offer. Examples are RESTAURANTS, PLUMBING, AIR-CONDITIONING, AUTO SALES, and PHYSICIANS.
2. These *headings*, showing the service, product, or specialty, are arranged *alphabetically*.
3. Under these headings, the names of the businesses appear in alphabetical order.
4. Each listing consists of the name, address, and telephone number, just as it does in the white pages. But these listings are under a heading. For example, Smith's Garage is not under "S" for Smith. It is under GARAGES or AUTOMOBILE SERVICE.
5. Many of these yellow page listings also appear as classified ads. These ads give more information about a business. They may give hours, location, and directions.

Activity 7

Answer these questions about the yellow pages.

Deciding when to use the yellow pages

1. If you are a shopper, what are some benefits of looking for a business in the yellow pages? (Name at least three.)_____

_____

_____

2. John Watts owns a foreign car. He needs to have it repaired. Should he look in the white pages or yellow pages for a repair shop?_____

3. You want Carlos' Foreign Car Repair to give your car a tune-up. You know where the repair shop is. But you need the telephone number to call for an appointment. Would you use the yellow pages or the white pages? Explain your answer._____

_____

Activity 8

Classifying yellow-page listings

Below are yellow page headings that deal with furniture and automobiles. These headings are lettered. Stores are also listed. Decide under which heading each store belongs.

a. FURNITURE DEALERS - RETAIL
b. FURNITURE RENTING & LEASING
c. FURNITURE REPAIRING & REFINISHING

_____ 1. Universal Refinishers

_____ 2. The Restore

_____ 3. Quality Furniture

_____ 4. Flex-A-Lease, Inc.

_____ 5. I.F.G. Furniture Rentals

_____ 6. Frank's Used Furniture Store

_____ 7. Modern Foam Furniture

_____ 8. American Furniture Rentals

_____ 9. Mitchell Upholstery

_____ 10. Imported Scandinavian Furniture

Now classify the car businesses listed below under the correct yellow page heading.

a. AUTOMOBILE BODY REPAIRING & PAINTING
b. AUTOMOBILE DEALERS - ANTIQUE & CLASSIC
c. AUTOMOBILE DEALERS - NEW CARS
d. AUTOMOBILE PARTS & SUPPLIES
e. AUTOMOBILE RADIOS & STEREO SYSTEMS

_____ 1. Smith's Foreign Car Parts

_____ 2. Clark Auto Parts, Inc.

_____ 3. Pierre's Classic Cars, Inc.

_____ 4. Vintage Vehicles, Inc.

_____ 5. Bob's Hubcap Specialists

_____ 6. J & G Automotive Parts

_____ 7. Dan's Body & Fender Shop

_____ 8. Dependable Auto Parts Store

_____ 9. A & E Auto Supply

_____ 10. George's Body Shop

_____ 11. Central Chevrolet

_____ 12. Autosound, Inc.

_____ 13. Glenbrook Ford, Inc.

_____ 14. Bill's Auto Painting

_____ 15. Sound Experience, Inc.

_____ 16. Chrysler-Plymouth Sales

Activity 9

Reading and understanding the yellow pages

Use these yellow page listings to answer the following questions.

1. What is the type of business found on this page?_____

2. What is the *first* alphabetical listing on this page?_____

3. What is the *last* alphabetical listing on this page?_____

4. Did any listings under the same heading come *before* this page?

_____

5. Are the businesses on this page providing products or a service?_____

Some of the listings give more than telephone numbers and addresses. These listings appear in boxes. They tell about the services and sometimes the hours of the business. They are called classified ad listings. Refer to these ads in answering the remaining questions.

6. What place cleans wedding gowns?_____

_____

7. Name three places that clean leather.

_____

_____

_____

8. Which cleaner replaces buttons?_____

_____

9. Which cleaner will take down your drapes?_____

Activity 10

Choosing the yellow pages or the white pages

Classify the items below according to where they are most likely found—YELLOW PAGES, WHITE PAGES, or BOTH.

a. WHITE PAGES
b. YELLOW PAGES
c. BOTH

_____ 1. Jones, Charles

_____ 2. Bambi Department Store

_____ 3. Acme Printing Company

_____ 4. Smith, T. J.

_____ 5. Chun King Restaurant

_____ 6. Posey, Ernest

_____ 7. Central Television Repair Shop

_____ 8. Consumer Complaints Department

_____ 9. Penn, Carolyn

_____ 10. Public Health Department

_____ 11. Robinson, Charles, M.D.

_____ 12. Poison Control Center

_____ 13. Lawson, E. J.

_____ 14. Lawson Brothers Realty

_____ 15. James, Fred

_____ 16. Jones Chemicals

_____ 17. Smith's Transfer

_____ 18. Chi Mer Restaurant

_____ 19. Wilson, John T. (attorney)

_____ 20. A & B Clothing

Reading the area code map

The United States is divided into telephone dialing areas. Each area has an area code. This is a three-digit number. You use this number to dial long distance. For example, you want to call 555-2364 in Florida. But you live in Utah. You must dial the area code first. It is 305. So you must dial 305 and then 555-2364. When you do not know an area code, you can use the area code map in your telephone book. This map gives you the area codes for the United States and Canada. More than 120 dialing areas appear on this map. The map also divides the United States into time zones. Notice that when it is 1:00 in California, it is 4:00 in Michigan.

Activity 11

Reading area code maps

Study the following area code map. Use this map to answer the questions below and on page 248.

1. Give the area codes for South Carolina_____   Wyoming_____

   South Dakota_____   Utah_____

13

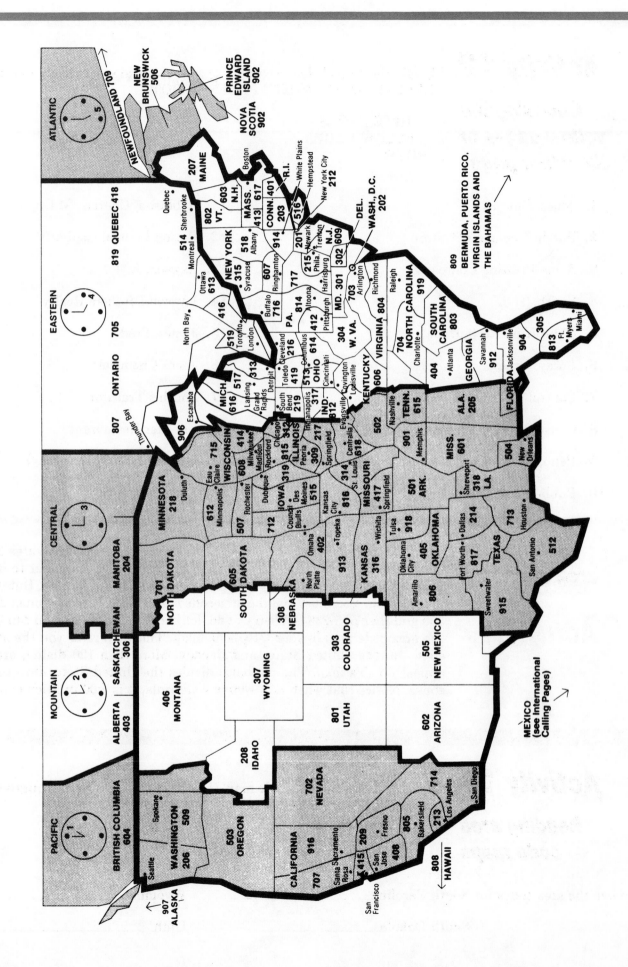

14

2. Give the area codes for Alaska_____   Bermuda_____

Hawaii_____   Puerto Rico_____

3. Give the area codes for Ontario, Canada_____

Quebec_____

Saskatchewan_____

4. How many dialing areas (area codes) are in the state of Florida?_____

West Virginia?_____

Georgia?_____

Montana?_____

Texas?_____

5. What city in Texas is in the 512 area?_____

the 713 area?_____

the 214 area?_____

6. If you wanted to make a long distance call to Philadelphia (Phila), Pennsylvania, from out of state, what area code would you dial before the number?_____

7. If you wanted to call Atlanta, Georgia, what area code would you dial?_____

Activity 12

Reading area code maps

The area code map is divided into five time zones. They are Pacific, Mountain, Central, Eastern, and Atlantic. Bold lines divide these geographical areas. Read each of the situations below. Decide which statement is correct. Also answer each time question.

Situation #1

You live in Seattle, Washington. At 9:01 A.M., you make a business call to New York City. You want to catch Jim Brown, the president of Lyons Construction, as soon as he arrives to work. The office hours are 9 to 5.

When you call, the secretary tells you:
_____ A Mr. Brown just left for lunch.
_____ B the office just opened and Mr. Brown should be in shortly.
_____ C the office is closing, call tomorrow.

What time is it in New York?_____

Situation #2

John Johnson calls his insurance company in Des Moines, Iowa. The person who answers the phone tells him that his agent, Mr. Brown, will be in at 3:00. John is calling from Maryland (MD). When John calls back, his watch has exactly 3:00.

But the receptionist tells him:
_____ A his agent is at lunch from 12 to 1:00.
_____ B call back at 4:00.
_____ C call back in an hour.

What time is it in Des Moines?_____

CHECK YOUR UNDERSTANDING OF THE TELEPHONE DIRECTORY

1. A listing for The Skillful Carpenter is under what letter in the white pages?_____

2. Under what heading in the yellow pages would you most likely find the Skillful Carpenter?

_____

3. Your foreign car needs repairs. What heading do you look up in the yellow pages?_____

4. How do you find a plumber in the yellow pages?_____

5. You want to call your friend, Jason Pierce. You look under the letter_____ in the white pages.

6. You live in Chicago, Illinois. You want to call your friend in Los Angeles, California at 8:30 in the morning, California time. What is the time in Chicago when you make the call?_____

7. You are at work in New York City. You place a business call to Houston, Texas. It is 1:00 P.M. in New York. In Houston:
_____ a. the work day is over
_____ b. it is the lunch hour
_____ c. the work day has not begun

8. Put the following names in alphabetical order. Names beginning with Mac or Mc are alphabetized letter by letter. So all the Mac's come before the Mc's.

McNeil_____   MacDonald_____

Miner_____   Mack_____

Major_____   McKay_____

9. What does the abbreviation, Pk, mean?_____

10. Why might Dr. Gilbert Brown, Dentist, have two numbers listed after his name in the white pages?_____

16

Special reading skills

Often information you need will require special reading skills. You may have to interpret a sign, symbol, or drawing. You may have to make comparisons using a chart or graph. You may have to read a schedule.

This chapter gives you practice in using everyday reference skills. First you learn how to identify street and highway signs. Then you read both street and highway maps. Transportation schedules and charts and graphs follow. You will practice reading, bus, train, and plane schedules. And you will interpret line, bar, and circle graphs. This chapter also shows you how to read your gas, electric, and telephone bills.

Street and highway signs

WORDS TO KNOW

guide signs signs that show exits, distances, and directions, such as route numbers

maximum speed the fastest speed allowed

minimum speed the slowest speed allowed

obstruction something that is blocking the road

pedestrian a person who is walking

posted sign a sign that is put in a place where it can be seen easily

regulatory signs signs that give information about traffic laws such as speed limits

right-of-way when a driver has the right to go first

service signs signs that point out services such as rest stops, telephones, and gas stations

warning signs signs that give warnings or cautions such as a low bridge or a sharp curve in the road

Street and highway signs carry important messages for drivers. They tell them the traffic laws. They warn of possible dangers ahead. They give distances and directions. They even direct drivers to telephones, gas stations, and rest stops.

Street and highway signs are grouped in three categories. They are REGULATORY SIGNS, WARNING SIGNS, and SERVICE AND GUIDE SIGNS.

Regulatory signs

These signs tell you speed limits and other traffic laws. Most regulatory signs are white with black letters.

Traffic in the right lane must turn right. Traffic in the left lane may go straight or turn right.

Drivers should keep to the right of an obstruction.

This sign is posted over a turning lane. Traffic from both directions uses this lane.

The fastest safe speed is 55 miles per hour. The minimum safe speed is 45 miles per hour.

These signs mark Passing and No Passing zones.

Sometimes a message on a regulatory sign is very important. This sign will be red with white letters.

This sign means come to a complete stop.

The driver *does not* have the right-of-way. Slow down and let right-of-way driver go first.

Don't drive onto any street or enter any highway with this sign.

You are driving the wrong way on a freeway, ramp, or street. You may meet another car.

A red circle with a line through it always means NO.

NO RIGHT TURN

NO TRUCKS

NO U TURN

Some regulatory signs are for pedestrians also. *No hitchhiking* is an example. Can you think of others?

Activity 1 Match the signs with their meanings.

Identifying regulatory signs

A.   B.  C.   D.

E.   F.   G.  H.

I.   J.

_____ **1.** No "U" turn.

_____ **2.** No trucks allowed.

_____ **3.** This sign means the opposite of "Go."

_____ **4.** Slow down. Be prepared to stop for right-of-way drivers.

_____ **5.** Turning lane.

_____ **6.** Stay out!

_____ **7.** Maximum safe speed is 55 m.p.h.

_____ **8.** You're driving in the wrong direction.

_____ **9.** Drivers should keep to the right of an obstruction.

_____ **10.** No right turn.

20

Warning signs
Warning signs are yellow with black letters. They're usually diamond-shaped.

Sharp curve ahead. Take curve at 35 mph.

Crossroads or side roads ahead. Watch for other vehicles entering, leaving, or crossing highways.

A bridge or underpass ahead. Clearance is 12 feet 6 inches.

Traffic light ahead. Be prepared to stop.

Traffic island or obstruction ahead. Drive to either side.

Reminder: two-way highway

Slow down and watch for schoolchildren.

Begin slowing down. You must stop soon.

A section of the highway is slippery when wet. Driver should slow down.

Traffic may be moving into your lane. Be ready to change speed or lane.

This means pedestrian crossing. Watch out for people walking across highway.

This means bicycle crossing. Watch out for people riding bicycles.

This sign warns of a hill where driver must take special care.

The unpaved edge of the road is soft. Stay on pavement.

Almost everyone has seen these two warning signs.

This No Passing Zone sign is usually followed by a black and white regulatory sign.

Train may be crossing highway. Slow down and be prepared to stop.

Activity 2 Match the signs with their meanings.

Identifying warning signs

A.

B.

C.

D.

E.

F.

G.

H.

I.

K.

_____ **1.** People crossing.

_____ **2.** Watch for bike riders.

_____ **3.** Watch out for schoolchildren.

_____ **4.** Highway ahead has two-way traffic.

_____ **5.** Watch for traffic moving into your lane.

_____ **6.** Side road ahead — watch for vehicles entering highway.

_____ **7.** Traffic light ahead. BE PREPARED TO STOP!

_____ **8.** Rail Road Crossing

_____ **9.** Curve ahead.

_____ **10.** Intersection ahead. Watch for vehicles entering, leaving, or crossing highway.

Service and guide signs

Service and guide signs are usually seen on major routes and interstate highways. These signs tell you what to expect ahead. Guide signs are white and green. They point out such things as exits, bike routes, and hiking trails.

They also give distances and directions:

Found in front of intersections, they show the direction to cities.

Used on main highways, these signs show distance.

Others identify routes by number, symbol, and shape. These routes are part of national, state, and local highway systems.

Interstate sign

U.S. Route markers

A State Highway sign for Michigan

Expressway Exit

On interstate highways and freeways you may see blue and white service signs. These signs direct you to rest rooms, telephones, restaurants, and gas stations. Sometimes you will see words *and* symbols. Sometimes you will only see symbols.

Rest stops

No handicap barriers

Route to nearest hospital

Location of picnic table

Signs showing state and local parks are usually brown with white letters or symbols.

Activity 3

Identifying street and highway signs

Label these signs as REGULATORY, WARNING, or SERVICE AND GUIDE.

_____

_____

_____

_____

_____

_____

CHECK YOUR UNDERSTANDING OF SIGNS

Tell the meaning of each of the following signs.

1. _____

2. _____

3. _____

4. _____

5. _____

6. _____

7. _____

8. _____

9. _____

10. _____

Reading maps

A map contains a lot of information important to drivers. A map can tell you the number of miles between cities. A map can direct you to interstate routes and U.S. highways. A map can help you get back on the right road when you are lost. Do you know how to read a map? Many people don't.

The first thing you must find on a map is *where you are*. The second thing is *where you are going.*

Map skills: where you are

A map usually has a directional symbol. It tells you which direction on the map is north, south, east, and west. North is usually at the top of the map. South is always opposite north. So south is usually at the bottom. West is to your left. East is to your right. Directional symbols are often called pointers. North is "N." South is abbreviated as "S." East is "E." West is abbreviated as "W."

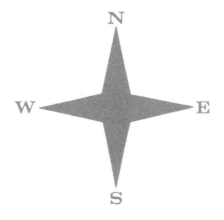

Your first job using any map is to find where you are. Study the following map.

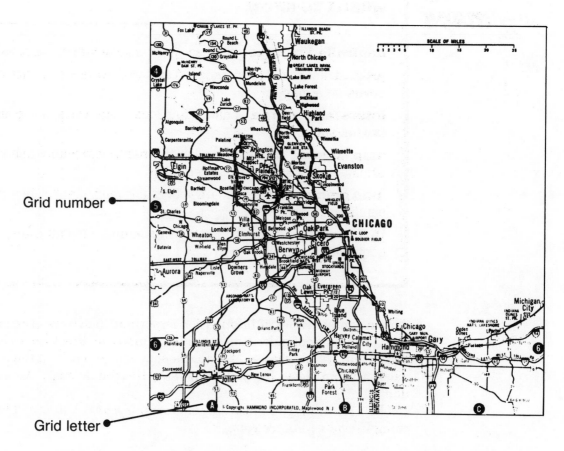

Grid number

Grid letter

Now look at the index to the Chicago area map.

CHICAGO METROPOLITAN AREA

A map index and a grid system help you read the map. The grid consists of numbers and letters. You find the town you're in on the map index. The index lists locations in alphabetical order. It also lists the grid points. Then you locate the grid points on the map. In the map above, Chicago, Illinois is where B and 5 meet. Grids for highway maps list cities. Grids for city maps list streets.

There are other ways to find where you are on a map. One is to use the map legend:

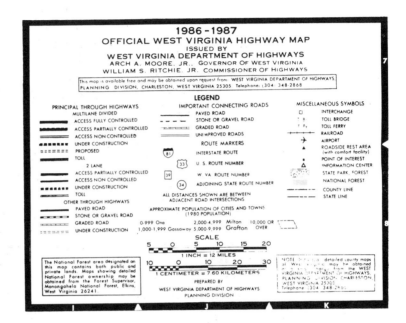

A map legend identifies symbols used on a map. Examples of symbols are those used to show highways. There are interstate, U.S., State, and local highways. The roads on the map are numbered. They are called routes. You can use the highway or route you're on to find where you are on a map. Legends often help identify parks, lakes, and other places of interest to travelers. Map symbols help you find these locations.

Map skills: where you are going

Once you've found your map location, you can find where you are going. You can use your finger as a marker. Trace the various routes to your destination. Will you travel interstate highways, state roads, or county and local roads? Will you travel north, south, or northwest? There is one thing you must remember. You must keep your directions in mind. Are you traveling south to north or north to south? In other words, are you traveling up the map or down the map? Are you going east, toward the right of the map? Are you going west, toward the left of the map? A right turn going up the map will be a left turn coming down.

Activity 4

Using map grids

This Michigan map has grid numbers and letters along the right side and the bottom. Use these grids to answer the questions below the map.

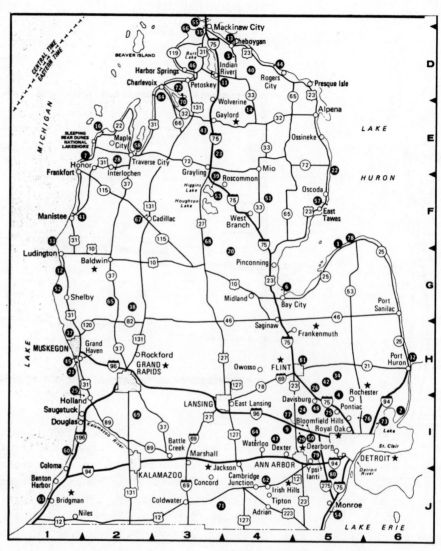

Indicate the map grids for the following Michigan cities.

1. Lansing_____

2. Grand Rapids_____

3. Detroit_____

4. Traverse City_____

5. Muskegon_____

Activity 5
Look over this map of Detroit. Then answer the questions that follow.

Using street maps

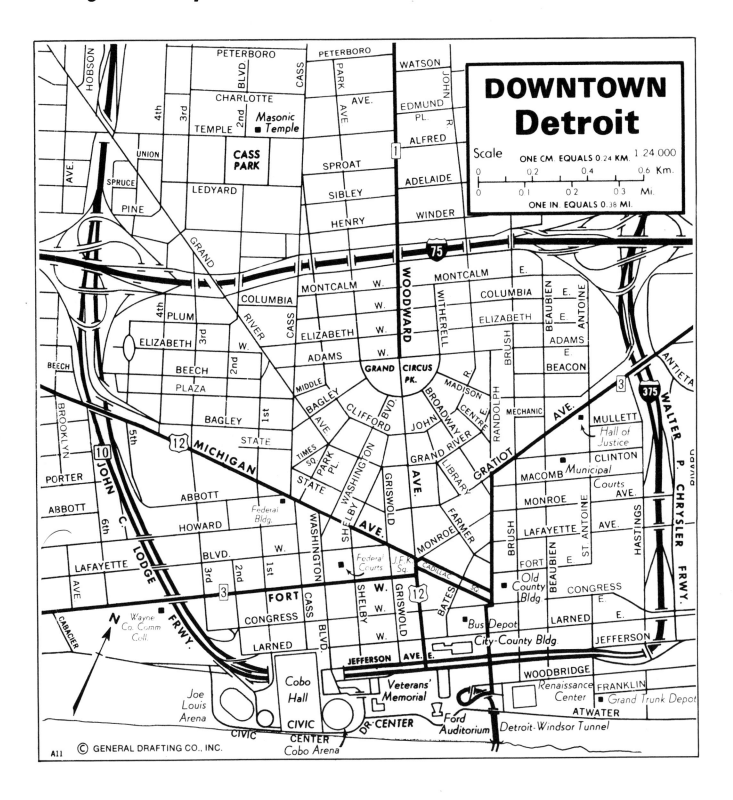

1. List the interstate highways in and around Detroit. _____

2. Is I-375 a north/south highway or an east/west highway? _____

3. Locate Fort Avenue near the bottom of the map. Take Fort Avenue to Woodward Avenue (Highway 12) and turn south. Travel Woodward south until you come to Larned Avenue. Turn east and drive to Beaubien. Travel north on Beaubien past Macomb and to the corner of Clinton and Beaubien. What public place are you near? _____

4. Locate Charlotte Avenue in the upper left portion of the map. Travel east on Charlotte Avenue to Cass and turn right. Take Cass to Michigan Avenue and travel southeast until it runs into Woodward Avenue. Take the first right off Woodward to Fort, and take Fort past the John C. Lodge Freeway.

   Name the educational institution on your left. _____

5. Describe the simplest route from the Bus Depot (lower right of map) to Cass Park. _____

   _____

   _____

   _____

6. Locate the Civic Center at the bottom of the map. List the public buildings that are part of the Civic

   Center area. _____

   _____

   _____

   _____

7. This map has a directional symbol. Which corner of the map contains this directional symbol?

   a. northwest corner _____

   b. southeast corner _____

   c. southwest corner _____

   d. northeast corner _____

CHECK YOUR UNDERSTANDING OF READING MAPS

Study this map of Baltimore, Maryland. Answer these questions about it.

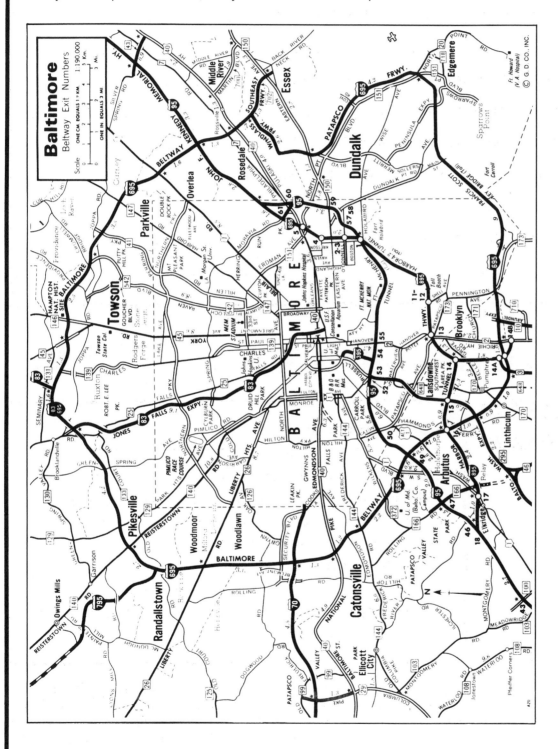

1. What interstate routes are in the Baltimore area? _____

2. List the two U.S. routes on the map. _____

3. Which highway is named after John F. Kennedy? _____

4. What are two ways to get from Dundalk to Brooklyn? _____

   _____

5. U.S. Route 1 to the northeast of Baltimore is also what street? _____

6. Is Pimlico Race Course shown on this map? _____

7. What highway is also called the Baltimore Beltway? _____

8. What state park is in the southwest corner of the map? _____

   _____

9. What is the most direct route from Arbutus to downtown Baltimore? _____

   _____

Transportation schedules

WORDS TO KNOW

A.M.   from midnight to noon (morning)

arrival time   the expected time you get where you are going

commuter   a person who travels back and forth regularly

departure time   the time of leaving

originating point   the place a trip starts

P.M.   from noon to midnight (afternoon and evening)

terminating point   the place a trip ends (last stop on bus, train, etc.)

What time will your train leave Charleston, West Virginia, for Washington, D.C.? Is there a morning bus to Hillside, New Jersey? Are there any evening flights out of Chicago, Illinois? There are many ways to travel. The most popular forms of public transportation are bus, train, and plane.

Being able to read a schedule can come in very handy. Schedules can help you get to work on time. They can make travel and vacations easier.

They can even help you plan your time. (A schedule can help keep you from being in the wrong place at the wrong time.) Schedules tell you when you'll get where you are going. Some schedules tell you all the stops along the way. Before you take a bus, train, or plane, you should know how to read a schedule.

Reading schedules

There are many types of transportation schedules. Examples are express, commuter, and tour schedules. To use schedules effectively, you must know what they have in common.

All schedules should show the originating point. And all schedules should show the terminating point. Most people refer to these as FROM and TO.

The bus schedule below only shows two points—originating and terminating. But some schedules show all points between these locations. These points are called stops.

All schedules should show departure times and arrival times.

Most schedules are read either down or across. This means that you may read across the schedule to locate your arrival time. Or you may read down the schedule to locate your arrival time. When there is only one place of departure and arrival, schedules usually read ACROSS.

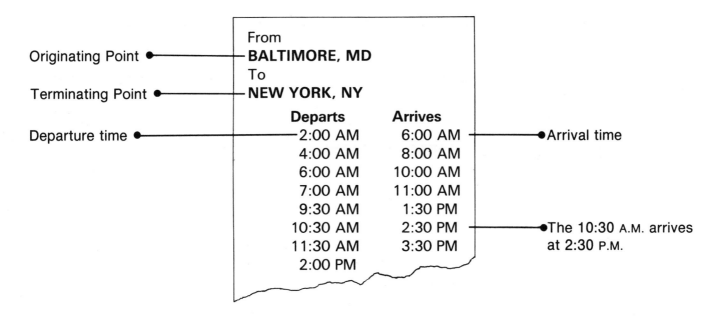

Originating Point •

Terminating Point •

Departure time •

From
BALTIMORE, MD
To
NEW YORK, NY

Departs	Arrives
2:00 AM	6:00 AM
4:00 AM	8:00 AM
6:00 AM	10:00 AM
7:00 AM	11:00 AM
9:30 AM	1:30 PM
10:30 AM	2:30 PM
11:30 AM	3:30 PM
2:00 PM	

• Arrival time

• The 10:30 A.M. arrives at 2:30 P.M.

In the sample above the column headings help you read this schedule. First you read your departure time under "Departs." Then you read across the same line. You locate your arrival time under "Arrives." Many transportation schedules have several columns. They also show many stops. You must study these schedules to determine how you should read them.

In the next schedule there are five columns showing departures. These show buses going from Baltimore to New York. These are buses #1, #2, #3, #4, and #5. They all make the same run. This schedule reads DOWN.

Read down
from Baltimore
to New York ●

Bus #3
Leaves at
12:00 noon ●

Arrives at ●
4:30 P.M.

From **BALTIMORE, MD** To **NEW YORK, NY**					
	#1 Sun	#2	#3	#4	#5
Baltimore, MD	9:00	8:00	**12:00**	**6:00**	2:00
Joppatowne, MD	—	8:15	**12:15**	**6:15**	2:15
Edgewood, MD	—	8:30	**12:30**	**6:30**	2:30
Aberdeen, MD	—	8:45	**12:45**	**6:45**	2:45
Havre de Grace, MD	—	9:00	**1:00**	**7:00**	3:00
Elkton, MD	—	9:30	**1:30**	**7:30**	3:30
Wilmington, DE	10:45	9:45	**1:45**	**7:45**	3:45
Newark, NJ	**1:00**	12:00	**4:00**	**10:00**	6:00
New York City	**1:30**	12:30	**4:30**	**10:30**	6:30
Notes: **P.M.—Boldface** Sun–Sundays only		All trips operate daily unless otherwise noted.			

Reading down, Bus #3 leaves from Baltimore at 12:00 noon. It goes through Joppatowne, Edgewood and so on until it arrives in New York City at 4:30 P.M. If you want to leave at 2:00 A.M., you locate the 2:00 A.M. bus (#5). You then read down to your destination for the arrival time. At the bottom of a schedule is a "notes" section. Abbreviations and symbols used are explained here. On many transportation schedules, this section is called the "key." Look at the "notes" section of this schedule.

The "notes" section tells you that buses that run between 12 noon and midnight are shown in boldface (dark) type. The symbols, A.M. and P.M. do not appear on the schedule. You must read the notes in order to get the time right for the bus you want to take. Also notice that bus #1 runs only on Sundays. It is possible to travel from Baltimore to New York City by bus on Sunday, but you must take the 9 A.M. bus. There are no other buses that day from Baltimore to New York.

Activity 6

Reading schedules down

The schedule below shows trains going from New York to Detroit. You have to read *down* this schedule to find stops (and departure times) between these two cities.

New York-Albany-Syracuse- Rochester-Buffalo-Niagara Falls-Detroit

		Train Number		63	69	73	71	75	65	49	79
		Train Name		The Niagara Rainbow	The Adirondack	The Empire State Express	The Henry Hudson	The Washingtonton Irving	The Salt City Express	The Lake Shore Limited	The DeWitt Clinton
		Frequency of Operation		Daily	Daily	Daily	Daily	Daily	Daily	Daily	Daily
		Type of Service		⊠ ▭	⊠	✓ ⊠	⊠	⊠	✓ ⊠	⇥ ✗ ▭	⊠
Km	Mi										
0	0	*(Conrail)* **New York, NY** *(ET)* *(Grand Central Terminal)*	Dp	8 40 A	9 15 A	12 40 P	2 40 P	4 40 P	5 40 P	6 40 P	8 40 P
53	33	Croton-Harmon, NY ⑮		R 9 37 A	R 10 03 A	R 1 28 P	R 3 28 P	R 5 28 P	R 6 28 P	R 7 37 P	R 9 28 P
119	74	Poughkeepsie, NY ⑮ *(Highland)*		R 10 21 A	R 10 48 A	R 2 13 P	R 4 13 P	R 6 13 P	R 7 13 P	R 8 21 P	R 10 13 P
143	89	Rhinecliff, NY *(Kingston)*		10 37 A	11 04 A	2 29 P	4 29 P	6 29 P	7 29 P	8 37 P	10 29 P
185	115	Hudson, NY		11 02 A	11 27 A	2 52 P	4 52 P	6 52 P	7 52 P	9 02 P	10 52 P
230	143	**Albany-Rensselaer, NY**	Ar		12 05 P	3 30 P	5 30 P	7 30 P	8 30 P	9 45 P	11 30 P
230	143		Dp	12 05 P		3 40 P			8 40 P	10 00 P	
245	152	Colonie-Schenectady, NY		12 26 P		3 55 P			8 55 P		
257	160	Schenectady, NY		㉙		㉙			㉙	㉙	
286	178	Amsterdam, NY		12 54 P		4 20 P			9 20 P		
383	238	**Utica, NY**		1 55 P		5 17 P			10 17 P	11 52 P	
406	252	Rome, NY *(Griffiss AFB)*		2 11 P		5 31 P			10 31 P		
460	286	**Syracuse, NY**		2 42 P		6 02 P			11 05 P	12 45 A	
599	372	**Rochester, NY**		4 15 P		7 32 P				2 20 A	
695	432	Cheektowaga, NY ㉙ ●									
705	438	Buffalo, NY *(Central Tml.)*		5 32 P		8 40 P				3 50 A	
708	440	**Buffalo, NY** *(Exchange St.)*	Ar	5 37 P		8 45 P					
748	465	**Niagara Falls, NY**		6 40 P		9 45 P					
938	583	St. Thomas, Ont. ●		9 28 P							
1115	693	Windsor, Ont. ● *(Amtrak Sta.)*		11 10 P							
1120	696	**Detroit, MI** *(Amtrak Sta.) (ET)*	Ar	11 30 P							

Answer these questions about the train schedule above.

1. How many trains appear on this schedule?_____

2. What are the numbers of these trains?_____

_____

3. What is the number of the train that goes all the way from New York to Detroit?_____

4. What is the name of the train referred to in question 3?_____

5. What time does this train leave New York?_____

6. What time does this train arrive in Detroit?_____

7. What is the last stop for the Henry Hudson?_____

   The Adirondack? _____

   The Washington Irving?_____

   The Lake Shore Limited?_____

Activity 7

Reading schedules across

As you read *across* the airline schedule on the next page, each column gives you information on a specific flight. (The codes and abbreviations used here would be explained at the bottom of the schedule.) You learn when a flight leaves and when a flight arrives. You learn a flight's number and how often a plane flies. Continuing to read across, you will find a column for connecting cities and one showing the stops a plane makes. Use this schedule to answer the questions below.

1. Determine the departure time, the arrival time, and the number of stops for each of these Asheville flights:

FROM ASHEVILLE, N.C.

TO	Flight #	Departure Time	Arrival Time	# of Stops
Augusta, Ga.	88/918	_____	_____	_____
Charleston, W.Va.	60	_____	_____	_____
Columbia, S.C.	88/918	_____	_____	_____

2. How many flights leave Asheville each day for

Atlanta, Ga.? _____

Chicago, Ill.? _____

Columbus, Ohio? _____

3. If you leave for Atlanta, Ga., at 9:52, you will be on what flight? _____

4. If you leave for Augusta, Ga., will you be on the same flight? _____

5. If you leave Asheville for Augusta, in what city will you have to make a connection? _____

6. What will be your flight number when you leave the connecting city for Columbus, Ohio? _____

7. Name at least four cities to which this airline has nonstop flights. _____

_____

_____

8. Flight #62 from Asheville to Fayetteville/Fort Bragg, N.C., operates daily except _____ .

Column 1–*Leave* = Time plane leaves Asheville, N.C.

Column 2–*Arrive* = Time plane arrives in desired city

Column 3–*Flight No.* = Number identifying a particular flight

1	2	3	4	5	6
Leave	Arrive	Flight-No.	Freq.	Connect Via	Stops
FROM ASHEVILLE, N. C.					
Reservations				254-4621	
TO					
ATLANTA, GA.					
8 30a	9 12a	**43**			0
9 52a	10 48a	**943**			0
1 35p	2 15p	**47**			0
4 25p	5 07p	**88**			0
9 35p	10 15p	**39**			0
AUGUSTA, GA.					
S 9 52a	12 50p	**943/914**		Atlanta	1
S 4 25p	6 25p	**88/918**	Ex Sa	Atlanta	1
S 4 25p	6 25p	**88/926**	Sa Only	Atlanta	1
CHARLESTON, W. VA.					
8 10a	8 52a	**60**			0
CHARLOTTE, N. C.					
5 44p	6 15p	**960**			0
CHICAGO, ILL.					
S 8 10a	11 39a ⓞ	**60/67**		Charleston	2
S 11 30a	12 38p ⓞ	**89**			1
S 2 30p	6 47p ⓞ	**10/81**		Roanoke	2
CINCINNATI, OHIO					
S 5 30p	9 46p	**24/927**		Winston-Salem	4
COLUMBIA, S. C.					
S 4 25p	7 01p	**88/918**	Ex Sa	Atlanta	2
S 4 25p	7 01p	**88/926**	Sa Only	Atlanta	2
COLUMBUS, OHIO					
8 10a	12 17p	**60/951**		Charleston	2
FAYETTEVILLE/FORT BRAGG, N. C.					
8 02a	9 14a	**72**			1
10 30p	11 10p	**62**	Ex Sa		0
GREENVILLE/SPARTANBURG, S. C.					
8 02a	8 23a	**72**			0
HICKORY/LENOIR/MORGANTON, N. C.					
7 34p	7 59p	**922**			0
HUNTINGTON, W. VA./ASHLAND, KY./IRONTON, OHIO					
8 10a	11 10a	**60/67**		Charleston	1
KINSTON/GOLDSBORO/GREENVILLE/CAMP LEJEUNE, N. C.					
5 44p	8 47p	**960/964**		Raleigh	2
KNOXVILLE/OAK RIDGE, TENN.					
11 14a	11 46a	**969**			0

Column 4–*Freq.* = Whether or not flights are daily. *Exceptions* appear here

Column 5–*Connect Via* = Name of the connect city, when you have to change planes

Column 6–*Stops* = Number of stops between "Leave" and "Arrive"

Activity 8
Reading terminal schedules

Airports post schedule information. They do this for flights arriving or departing from their terminals. They show flight numbers. They also show departure and arrival times for these flights. This information usually appears on a screen or board. Some airports show destinations and gate numbers. They may also show whether a plane is delayed, on time, or boarding.

ARRIVALS

Time	Flight #	Gate	From	Comments
2:15	72	7	Detroit	Arrived
2:20	174	9	Chicago	Landing
2:45	49	10	Houston	On Time
2:50	74	6	Dallas	On Time
3:00	711	5	Los Angeles	Delayed
3:10	80	4	Roanoke	On Time
3:15	39	3	Houston	On Time
3:20	63	2	Boston	On Time

TIME 2:17

DEPARTURES

Time	Flight #	Gate	To	Comments
3:10	71	33	Cleveland	Boarding
3:20	412	36	Boston	On Time
3:30	576	34	San Francisco	On Time
3:45	232	35	Dallas/Ft. Worth	On Time
4:00	109	39	Chicago	On Time
4:10	57	41	Detroit	On Time
4:15	74	32	Memphis	Delayed

TIME 3:06

Answer these questions about the schedules above.

1. What time is flight 80 scheduled to arrive?_____Will it be on time?_____

2. What time is flight 711 scheduled to arrive?_____Will it be on time?_____

3. Which flight arrives at Gate 10?_____   Gate 6?_____   Gate 3?_____

4. You have to meet a friend arriving from Chicago at 2:20. It is 2:17. Has the plane arrived?_____

5. What time is flight 74 scheduled to leave for Memphis?_____Will it leave on time?_____

6. Is flight 71 to Cleveland delayed?_____

7. Are passengers boarding flight 71 to Cleveland?_____If so, what gate are they using?_____

8. What is the flight number of the 3:20 flight to Boston?_____

9. Where is flight 57 scheduled to go?_____

Activity 9

Reading schedules up and down

Some schedules must be read down one side and up the other. The names of the stops are centered. And schedule information is on both sides.

In this schedule you read down to find departure times for buses going in one direction (Ocean City, MD). You read up the opposite side to find departure times for buses going in the opposite direction (Philadelphia, PA). Like all transportation schedules, this schedule shows arrival and departure times as either A.M. or P.M. In this schedule, A.M. is in lightface type, P.M. is in boldface (heavier) type. Other special information is explained at the bottom of the schedule.

Answer the questions about this interstate bus schedule.

NEW YORK PHILADELPHIA REHOBOTH BEACH OCEAN CITY

READ DOWN									READ UP			
				No.	**7303** 9-21-81		No. POC					
			5 30	**2 00**	Lv ▲**Philadelphia, PA**....♦...**CCC**... Ar	1135	**3 35**	**7 35**				
			6 05	**2 30**	▲Chester, PA............♦...(7300).	1100	**3 00**	**7 00**				
			6 35	**3 00**	▲**Wilmington, DE** 318 N. Market.	1035	**2 35**	**6 35**				
			6 50	**3 15**	Ar▲State Road, DE.........**CCC**... Lv	1020	**2 20**	**6 20**				
			3 00	1 00	Lv NEW YORK, NY...(7909)**TWI**... Ar	I 00	**4 50**	**8 35**				
			6 50	**3 25**	Ar State Road, DE......(7909)**TWI**... Lv	1010	**2 25**	**6 10**				
			7 05	**3 35**	Lv▲State Road, DE.............. Ar	1005	**2 05**	**5 55**				
			7 40	d	▲Smyrna....................	9 28	ss	**5 32**				
			8 00	**4 25**	▲**Dover**...................	9 10	**1 15**	**5 00**				
			8 25	**4 55**	Ar▲Harrington.........(7300)...... Lv	8 40	**12**⊛**45**	**4 30**				
			8⊛25	**4 55**	Lv▲Harrington.........(7301)...... Ar	8 40	**12 40**	**4 30**				
			8 40		Ar▲Milford...........(7300)...... Lv		**12 25**	**4 35**				
			8 40		Lv▲Milford...........(7301)...... Ar		**12 25**	**4 35**				
			d		Lewes....................	11 40						
			9 25		Ar▲**Rehoboth Beach**......... Lv	11 30						
			9 45		▲Bethany Beach, DE..........	11 05						
				5 55	Ar▲Salisbury, MD....(7300)...... Lv	7 40		**3**⊛**25**				
				6⊛00	Lv▲Salisbury, MD....(7301)...... Ar	7 35		**3 25**				
			1005	6 50	Ar▲**Ocean City, MD**......**CCC**... Lv	6 45	10 45	**2 45**				
				Mi.			Mi.					

Reference Marks for Tables 7301, 7303 and 7307
X—No local passengers carried between these points.

Sun—Sundays only.
Fri—Fridays only.
hs—Highway stop.
f—Flag stop.
d—Discharge passengers only.
N—No interstate service.
♦—Interstate service only.
POC—Thru Philadelphia-Ocean City.

B—Via Baltimore.
ss—Station stop.
OC—On Call.

All trips operate daily unless otherwise noted.
AM—Light Face.　　　**PM—Bold Face.**
Times shown in ITALICS indicate service via connecting trip or trips.

1. This schedule shows buses connecting what two main points?_____

2. If you were traveling from Chester, PA to Ocean City, MD, would you read *up* or *down* the schedule?_____

3. If you were traveling from Ocean City, MD to Chester PA, would you read *up* or *down* the schedule?_____

4. What time does the bus that leaves Philadelphia at 5:30 arrive in Ocean City?_____

5. What time is this bus scheduled to leave Chester, PA?_____

Wilmington, DE?_____

6. What time is this bus scheduled to arrive at the State Road stop in

Delaware?_____

Harrington, DE?_____

Milford, DE?_____

7. If you left Philadelphia at 2:00 in the afternoon, at what stop would you connect with the bus going

to Ocean City?_____

8. List all the stops between Ocean City and Philadelphia in the order that they come. Assume that the Ocean City bus makes every stop.

1st STOP_____   6th STOP_____

2nd STOP_____   7th STOP_____

3rd STOP_____   8th STOP_____

4th STOP_____   9th STOP_____

5th STOP_____   10th STOP_____

11th STOP_____

12th STOP_____

9. If you left New York on the 3:00 bus, what time would you arrive at the State Road stop in Delaware?_____

10. What time does the 5:30 bus out of Philadelphia arrive at the State Road stop in Delaware?_____

CHECK YOUR UNDERSTANDING OF SCHEDULES

The schedule below shows the train going from Salt Lake City to Seattle. And it shows the train from Seattle to Salt Lake City. You read down the left side of the schedule to find departure times for trains going to Seattle. These trains are traveling westward. You read up the opposite side of the schedule to find departure times for trains going to Salt Lake City. These trains are traveling eastward.

The Pioneer

Salt Lake City
Ogden
Boise
Portland
Seattle

READ DOWN						READ UP
25				Train Number		**26**
Daily				Frequency of Operation		Daily
🛏 ☒ 👜				Type of Service		🛏 ☒ 👜
	Km	Mi		*(Union Pacific)*		
11 25 P	0	0	Dp	**Salt Lake City, UT** *(Amtrak Sta.) (MT)*	Ar	7 10 A
12 20 A	58	36	Ar	**Ogden, UT**	Dp	6 10 A
12 35 A	58	36	Dp		Ar	5 55 A
F 1 05 A	92	57		Brigham City, UT •		F 5 25 A
3 20 A	276	170	Ar	**Pocatello, ID**	Dp	3 10 A
3 30 A	276	170	Dp		Ar	3 00 A
5 15 A	447	278		Shoshone, ID •		1 10 A
F 6 30 A	576	358		Mountain Home, ID •		F 11 55 P
7 30 A	650	404		**Boise, ID**		10 50 P
8 10 A	682	424		Nampa, ID • *(Caldwell)*		10 10 P
8 50 A	750	466		Ontario, OR • *(MT)*		9 30 P
9 50 A	890	553		Baker, OR • *(PT)*		6 30 P
11 10 A	975	606		La Grande, OR •		5 30 P
1 30 P	1094	680		Pendleton, OR •		3 10 P
2 05 P	1144	711		Hinkle, OR • *(Hermiston)*		2 35 P
3 35 P	1302	809		The Dalles, OR •		1 00 P
F 4 10 P	1339	832		Hood River, OR •		F 12 30 P
5 50 P	1440	895	Ar	**Portland, OR**	Dp	11 10 A
6 00 P	1440	895	Dp		Ar	11 00 A
				(Burlington Northern)		
6 21 P	1456	905		Vancouver, WA		10 33 A
7 00 P	1519	944		Kelso-Longview, WA		9 55 A
7 45 P	1588	987		Centralia, WA		9 06 A
8 05 P	1619	1006		East Olympia, WA •		8 46 A
8 50 P	1675	1041		Tacoma, WA		8 06 A
9 50 P	1740	1081	Ar	**Seattle, WA** *(King St. Sta.) (PT)*	Dp	7 10 A

The Pioneer
Salt Lake City-Seattle

Services

Amfleet Service

Tray Meal and Beverage Service—*Am-dinette*
Sleeping Car Service—Complimentary coffee and tea served on request 6:30-9:30 AM.
Coach Service—Reserved and unreserved seats.
Baggage Service—Checked baggage handled at Ogden, Pocatello, Boise, Portland and Seattle.

Answer these questions about this schedule. Read *down* the schedule.

1. What is the name of this train?____________________

2. What is the number of this train when it is going from Salt Lake to Seattle?__________

Seattle to Salt Lake?__________

3. What time does this train leave Salt Lake City for Seattle?__________

4. What time does this train arrive in Ogden?__________

5. What time does it leave Ogden?_____

6. What time does this train leave La Grande, OR?_____

                         Pendelton, OR?_____

                         Portland, OR?_____

                         Vancouver, WA?_____

7. What time is the train scheduled to arrive in Seattle?_____

Answer these questions about this schedule. This time read *up* the schedule.

1. What time does the train leave Seattle for Salt Lake City?_____

2. What is the first stop after Seattle?_____

                         the second?_____

                         the third?_____

3. What time does the train arrive in Portland?_____

4. What time does it leave Portland?_____

5. What is the stop before Nampa, ID?_____

                         Boise, ID?_____

                         Pocatello, ID?_____

6. What is the stop before Salt Lake City?_____

7. What time is this train due to arrive in Salt Lake City?_____

Charts and graphs

WORDS TO KNOW

bar graph a graph showing changes by means of several broad lines called bars

chart information usually in the form of tables of numbers

circle graph a graph used to show the relation of the parts of anything to the whole

equivalent equal to

graph a drawing used to present numerical information clearer and easier

horizontal flat, parallel with the horizon, running across, level

line graph a graph showing numerical changes by means of narrow lines

vertical straight up and down

Some information can be found more quickly if it appears in a chart or graph. A *chart* is like a data table. It lists information. It also helps you make comparisons.

ANNUAL FUEL COSTS CHART

Dollars Per Gallon

ESTIMATED MPG	1.40	1.30	1.20	1.10	1.00	0.90	0.80
50	$420	$390	$360	$330	$300	$270	$240
49	428	398	367	337	304	275	245
48	437	406	374	343	312	281	250
47	447	415	383	351	320	288	256
46	456	423	391	358	326	293	260
45	466	433	400	366	333	300	266
44	477	443	409	375	340	306	272
43	489	454	419	384	350	315	280
42	500	464	428	393	357	321	286
41	512	476	439	403	366	329	293
40	525	488	450	412	375	338	300
39	538	499	461	422	384	346	307
38	552	513	473	434	394	355	316
37	567	526	486	446	405	364	324
36	584	542	500	459	417	375	334
35	601	558	515	472	429	386	343
34	617	573	529	485	441	397	353
33	636	591	545	500	454	409	364
32	655	608	562	515	468	421	374
31	678	630	581	533	484	436	388
30	699	649	599	549	500	450	400
29	724	673	621	569	518	466	414
28	750	696	643	589	536	482	428
27	777	722	666	610	555	500	444
26	808	751	693	635	578	520	462
25	840	780	720	660	600	540	480
24	876	813	751	688	626	563	500
23	914	848	783	718	652	587	522
22	956	887	819	751	682	614	546
21	1000	928	857	785	714	643	571
20	1050	975	900	825	750	675	600
19	1105	1026	947	868	789	710	631
18	1168	1084	1001	917	834	751	667
17	1235	1147	1058	970	882	794	706
16	1312	1219	1125	1031	938	844	750
15	1401	1301	1201	1101	1000	900	800
14	1499	1392	1285	1178	1071	964	857
13	1615	1500	1384	1269	1154	1038	923
12	1749	1624	1499	1374	1250	1125	1000
11	1909	1773	1636	1500	1364	1227	1091
10	2100	1950	1800	1630	1500	1350	1200
9	2333	2166	2000	1833	1666	1500	1333
8	2625	2438	2250	2062	1875	1688	1500
7	3001	2787	2572	2358	2144	1929	1715
6	3501	3251	3031	2751	2500	2250	2000
5	4200	3900	3600	3300	3000	2700	2400

The chart above shows annual fuel costs. Different cars get different gas mileage. This chart shows the cost of gasoline for one year. It shows this based on the average number of miles a car gets per gallon of gas. The miles per gallon (MPG) are shown vertically. They are on the left side of the chart. The cost of gasoline is shown horizontally. "Dollars Per Gallon" appears across the top of the chart. Let's say you car gets about 36 miles to a gallon. You locate "36" in the vertical column labeled ESTIMATED MPG. Then you read across the top of the chart. You find what you pay for gasoline. If you pay $1.30 per gallon, your annual fuel cost is $542.

Graphs give information too. Look at the graph below. It shows the annual attendance at the local zoo.

ATTENDANCE AT LOCAL ZOO

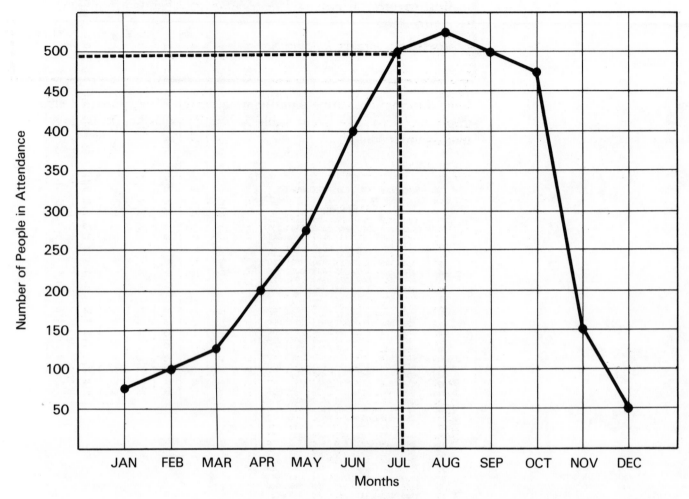

The vertical line shows the number of people in attendance. It is divided into units of 50 through 500. The horizontal axis shows the months of the year. You plot information on the graph. You do this by locating the point where the horizontal and vertical lines meet. The horizontal point shows the month. The vertical point shows the number of people at the zoo. In July there were 500 people in attendance at the local zoo.

You form the lines on the graph by connecting the dots. Each dot represents attendance for a given month. This type of graph is a line graph.

Activity 10

Reading a temperature chart

On the next page is a temperature chart. It is from the records of the U.S. Weather Bureau. It gives the average high and low temperatures for three states. They are Georgia, North Carolina, and South Carolina. Study the chart. Then answer the questions.

Temperature Averages - Maximum/Minimum
From the records of the National Weather Service

	JAN.	FEB.	MAR.	APR.	MAY	JUNE	JULY	AUG.	SEPT.	OCT.	NOV.	DEC.
GEORGIA												
Atlanta	54/36	57/37	63/41	72/50	81/59	87/66	88/69	88/68	83/63	74/52	62/40	53/35
Augusta	59/36	62/37	67/43	77/50	84/59	91/67	91/70	91/69	87/64	78/52	68/40	59/35
Columbus	59/37	61/38	67/43	76/51	85/60	91/68	92/71	91/70	87/65	78/53	67/42	59/36
Macon	60/38	63/39	69/45	78/53	87/61	93/69	93/71	92/70	88/65	79/54	68/43	60/38
Savannah	63/41	64/42	70/47	77/54	85/62	90/69	91/71	91/71	86/67	78/56	69/46	63/40
NORTH CAROLINA												
Asheville	49/30	51/31	57/36	68/44	76/53	83/60	85/64	74/63	79/57	69/46	57/36	50/30
Cape Hatteras	52/40	54/40	58/44	66/52	75/61	82/69	84/72	84/72	80/68	71/59	63/50	55/42
Charlotte	53/33	56/34	62/39	72/49	80/58	88/66	89/69	88/68	83/62	74/50	63/39	53/33
Raleigh	52/31	54/32	61/38	72/47	79/56	86/64	87/68	88/67	82/60	73/48	62/38	52/31
Winston-Salem	50/32	52/32	59/37	70/47	79/56	87/65	88/68	87/67	81/62	72/49	60/38	50/32
SOUTH CAROLINA												
Charleston	59/44	60/44	65/50	73/58	81/66	86/73	88/75	82/75	83/70	75/61	66/50	59/44
Columbia	58/36	61/36	67/42	76/51	85/60	92/70	93/71	92/70	86/65	77/52	67/41	58/35
Florence	58/37	60/37	67/43	76/51	84/60	90/68	91/70	90/70	85/64	77/53	67/43	58/36
Spartanburg	53/35	55/35	62/40	72/50	81/59	88/67	89/69	88/68	82/63	73/52	62/41	53/34

Note: Maximum temperatures appear above the line
Minimum temperatures appear below the line

1. What is the maximum average temperature in Atlanta, Georgia in January?_____

2. What is the minimum average temperature in Atlanta, Georgia in January?_____

3. What is the maximum average temperature in Macon, Georgia in July?_____

4. During which month does Columbus, Georgia have its lowest temperature?_____

5. During which month does Raleigh, North Carolina have its highest temperature?_____

6. Which city has the highest temperature in August—Charleston, South Carolina or Florence, South Carolina?_____

7. Of the cities listed, which one has the lowest temperature in January?_____

8. Of the cities listed, which one has the highest temperature in January?_____

Activity 11 Use this chart of recreation areas to answer the questions below.

Locating a recreation site

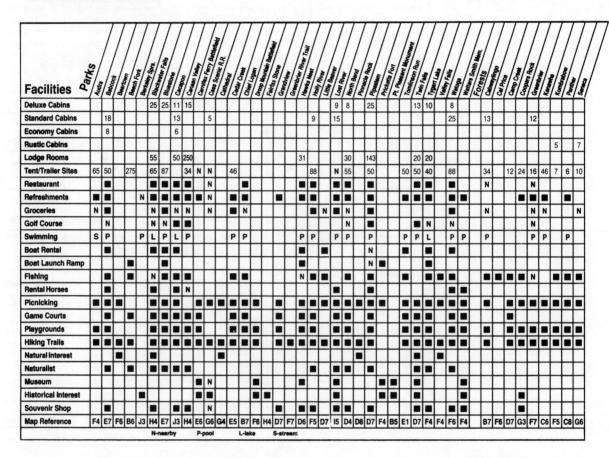

1. If you want to know which parks have a particular feature (for example, hiking trails), would you read *down* this chart or *across*? _____

2. If you want to know which features a particular park has (for example, Bluestone), would you read *down* this chart or *across*? _____

3. Does Grandview have cabins? _____

4. List the parks with boat ramps. _____

_____

5. Which parks have lakes? _____

_____

6. How is a "nearby" facility shown on this chart? _____

Activity 12

Reading a line graph

How did the track team do with its potato chip sales? How many cases of popcorn did the cheerleaders sell? What is the best month for popcorn sales? What is the best month for potato chips? Use the information plotted on this line graph to answer the questions below.

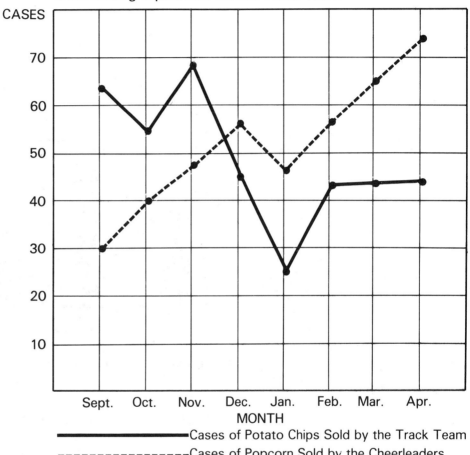

POPCORN & POTATO CHIP SALES:
Cheerleading Squad and School Track Team

───────── Cases of Potato Chips Sold by the Track Team

▪ ▪ ▪ ▪ ▪ ▪ ▪ ▪ ▪ Cases of Popcorn Sold by the Cheerleaders

1. Which group had the highest sales in the month of September?_____

2. Which group had the highest sales in the month of January?_____

3. How many cases of popcorn did the cheerleaders sell in March?_____

4. How many cases of potato chips did the track team sell in November?_____

5. Which group had the lowest-selling month?_____

   the highest-selling month?_____

6. The sales program came to an end in April. Which group was making the most sales by the end of the

   selling program?_____

Activity 13

Reading a bar graph

Another type of graph is the bar graph. Here is an example of a bar graph.

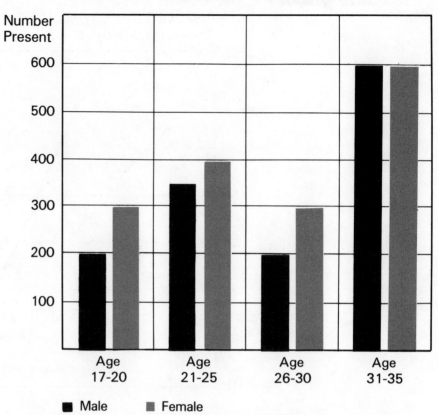

THEATRE ATTENDANCE — MAY 5

Use the graph to answer these questions.

1. How many females between 17 and 20 attended the theatre on May 5?_____

2. How many males between 17 and 20?_____

3. Which age group had the highest attendance on May 5?_____

4. What was the total attendance for the 26 to 30 age group?_____

5. Which age group, including male and female, had more than 500 present?_____

6. Which groups had the same overall attendance on May 5? _____

7. What was the total attendance for the 17-20 age group on May 5?_____

8. On May 5, did more males or more females attend the theatre?_____

50

Activity 14

Reading a circle graph

A circle graph shows the relationship of parts to a whole. You can divide a circle into sections. Then you can compare one section with another. You can also compare one section with the whole circle. Look at the budget circle below.

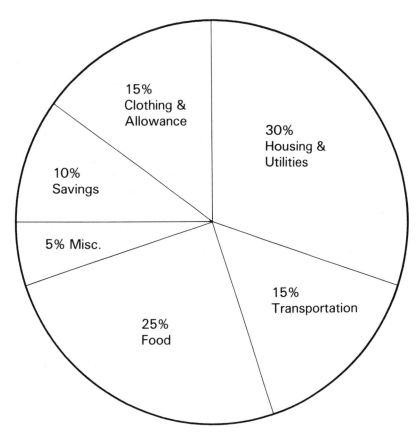

It shows how the Jacksons, a family of three, spend their yearly income. The questions that follow are about the Jacksons' budget circle. Choose the letter that correctly answers each question.

_____ 1. How much of the Jacksons' budget goes toward housing and utilities?
a. 10%
c. 30%
b. 20%
d. 40%

_____ 2. How much do they spend on savings?
a. 10%
c. 30%
b. 20%
d. 5%

_____ 3. Which two sections make up a little more than half of the Jacksons' budget?
a. Savings and Food
b. Food and Transportation
c. Miscellaneous (Misc.) and Food
d. Housing & Utilities and Food

_____ 4. Which section is the smallest part of the budget?
a. Transportation
b. Miscellaneous (Misc.)
c. Food
d. Clothing & Allowances

_____ 5. If the Jacksons' budget got too tight, which of these items could they eliminate?
a. Housing & Utilities
b. Food
c. Transportation
d. Savings

Study this chart of metric equivalents. This chart changes miles to kilometers. Answer the questions about it.

METRIC EQUIVALENTS

MILES (MPH)	CONVERSION TABLE	MILES TO KILOMETERS		MILES PER HOUR (MPH) TO KILOMETERS PER HOUR (km/h)					
		1	2	3	4	5	6	7	8	9
	KILO-METERS (km/h)	1.6	3.2	4.8	6.4	8.0	9.7	11.3	12.9	14.5
10	16.1	17.7	19.3	20.9	22.5	24.1	25.7	27.4	29.0	30.6
20	32.2	33.8	35.4	37.0	38.6	40.2	41.8	43.5	45.1	46.7
30	48.3	49.9	51.5	53.1	54.7	56.3	57.9	59.5	61.2	62.8
40	64.4	66.0	67.6	69.2	70.8	72.4	74.0	75.6	77.2	78.8
50	80.5	82.1	83.7	85.3	86.9	88.5	90.1	91.7	93.3	94.9
60	96.6	98.2	99.8	101.4	103.0	104.6	106.2	107.8	109.4	111.0
70	112.7	114.3	115.9	117.5	119.1	120.7	122.3	123.9	125.5	127.1
80	128.7	130.4	132.0	133.6	135.2	136.8	138.4	140.0	141.6	143.6
90	144.8	146.5	148.1	149.7	151.3	152.9	154.5	156.1	157.7	159.3
100	160.9									
200	321.9									
300	482.8									
400	643.7									
500	804.7									
1000	1609.4									

MILES TO KILOMETERS CONVERSION
(1 statute mile = 1.60935 kilometers)
Example: To find how many kilometers are equivalent to 65 miles, read DOWN to 60 miles in the left column, then RIGHT to 5 miles (fifth column). There are 104.6 kilometers in 65 miles.

The same reading converts MPH to km/h.

1. How many kilometers are in one mile?_____

2. How do you find kilometers per hour (km/h) if you know the miles per hour (MPH)?_____

_____

3. How many kilometers are there in 55 miles?_____

4. How many kilometers are there in 200 miles?_____

5. How many kilometers are there in 5 miles?_____

6. How many km/h are in 70 MPH?_____

7. How many km/h are in 35 MPH?_____

8. How many kilometers are there in 42 miles?_____

9. How can you convert kilometers to miles?_____

10. How many miles are there in 10 kilometers?_____

Utility bills

WORDS TO KNOW
CCF one hundred cubic feet, a measure of use of natural gas
disconnect to turn off
KWH kilowatt hour, one thousand watts of electricity used for one hour. A watt is a unit of electric power.
MCF one thousand cubic feet, a measure of use of natural gas
meter device for measuring and recording the amount of something
usage the amount of a utility consumed in a specific period of time

Utilities are a necessary part of every household. Gas, water, and electricity are utilities.

To bill you, a utility company reads a meter. The meter tells how much you used their service. Then you get a bill for each utility you use. Most utility companies bill customers each month.

Gas bills   Here is a sample gas bill:

BLUEFIELD GAS COMPANY						CASHIER'S STUB	
602 Raleigh			**Box 267**				
OFFICE HOURS 8:30 A. M. to 5:00 P. M. MONDAY THRU FRIDAY			PHONE Office 327-7161 Service 325-9164				

METER READING PER 100 CU. FT			Amount	Code	Date	AMOUNT	CODE
Previous	Present	Used					
783	788	5	15.39		7/28/88	15.39	TL

AFTER 10th OF MONTH ADD PN

NATURAL GAS RATES
SCHEDULE "A"

	Per Month			Per 100 Cu. Ft
First	200	Cu. Ft.	....	$0.515
Next	800	" "	....	0.215
Next	2,000	" "	....	0.165
Next	2,000	" "	....	0.135
Next	5,000	" "	....	0.115
Next	10,000	" "	....	0.105
Next	10,000	" "	....	0.095
Next	20,000	" "	....	0.090
All Over 50,000		" "	....	0.085
MINIMUM MONTHLY			....	1.00

Please Pay TL

F A—Fuel Adjustment
P N—Penalty
MD—Merchandise
AR—Arrears
TL—Total

Gas usage is shown in cubic feet. This bill shows every one hundred cubic feet as one unit of usage. The bill shows the number of units used by this customer. It also tells the customer the reading on the meter.

Activity 15

Complete these statements about the Bluefield Gas Company bill.

Reading gas bills

1. The previous meter reading for this customer was _____ .

2. This month's reading is _____ .

3. This means this customer used _____ units of gas for this billing period.

4. The bill is $ _____ .

5. A _____ charge will be added after the tenth of August.

6. If a customer uses less than 200 cubic feet of gas, the customer still must pay a minimum monthly charge of $ _____ .

7. If there is a question about this bill, the customer should call _____ .

8. If this customer needs to have the line checked for a leak, he or she should call _____ .

9. If the letters FA appear on a Bluefield Gas Company bill, they stand for a _____ cost.

10. Is the Bluefield Gas Company open on Saturday? _____

Electric bills

Information on an electric bill is similar to that on a gas bill. But your electricity is measured in KWHs, or kilowatt hours, instead of cubic feet (MCFs or CCFs). A kilowatt hour is 1000 watts used for a period of one hour. If you used a 1000-watt motor for one hour, you used one kilowatt hour. If you burned a 100-watt bulb for ten hours, then you also used one kilowatt hour (100×10).

Activity 16

Reading an electric bill

Answer the questions about the electric bill below. This bill also serves as a disconnect notice to the customer.

FOR BILL INFORMATION
DURING BUSINESS HOURS CALL: 253-7331

ACCOUNT NUMBER: (PLEASE USE WHEN YOU CALL OR WRITE)
2 011 11 10824 0 5

SERVICE NAME AND LOCATION:
WRIGHT WARREN W
300 CAWLEY ST
BECKLEY WV 25801

RATE SCHEDULE: RATES AVAILABLE ON REQUEST
015 RESIDENTIAL SERVICE

DISCONNECT NOTICE

| SERVICE PERIOD | | DEMAND | METER READINGS | | | | MULTIPLIER | KWH USED |
FROM	TO		PREVIOUS	CODE	PRESENT	CODE		
0910	100987		62590		63152		1	562

Electric service will be disconnected without further notice if PREVIOUS BALANCE is not paid on or before the "LAST PAY DATE" shown on this bill.

After this date the total amount of this bill is due, and if disconnected a reconnection charge must be paid for service to be restored. A cash security deposit may also be required prior to reconnection.

If you have already paid the PREVIOUS BALANCE shown on this bill, please accept our thanks.

DESCRIPTION	AMOUNT	CODE
BALANCE AS OF LAST BILLING DATE	49.56	
PREVIOUS BALANCE	49.56	
562 KWH USED THIS PERIOD	24.19	
LOCAL B & O TAX	1.05	
LOCAL UTILITY TAX	.50	
TOTAL	75.30	

CODES:
EST - ESTIMATED
MC - METER CHANGE
CR - CREDIT

| SETTLEMENT MONTH | EQUAL PAYMENT PLAN CUSTOMER | | LAST PAY DATE | AFTER LAST PAY DATE ADD | PAY THIS AMOUNT |
	MONTHLY AMT.	PREV. BALANCE			
			NOV 03		75.30

2011111082405

$.83 AVERAGE COST A DAY NOT INCLUDING TAX

AMERICAN ELECTRIC (AEP) POWER SYSTEM **APPALACHIAN POWER COMPANY**

1. How much does this customer owe the Appalachian Power Company? _____

2. How much of this amount is from a previous bill? _____

3. How many KWHs did the customer use this billing period? _____

4. Is this customer's meter read every month or every two months? _____

5. How much does the customer have to pay in B & O tax? _____

Your telephone bills

Many people feel that a telephone is just as important as electricity or gas. To them, having a telephone is a necessary part of running a household. The telephone company, like the utility companies, bills customers every month. But the telephone company does not read a meter. Charges are based on (1) how often you use your phone and (2) the type of calls you make. Study the following bill before doing Activity 17.

Sample phone bill
SHOWING BILL AND ITEMIZED CALLS STATEMENT

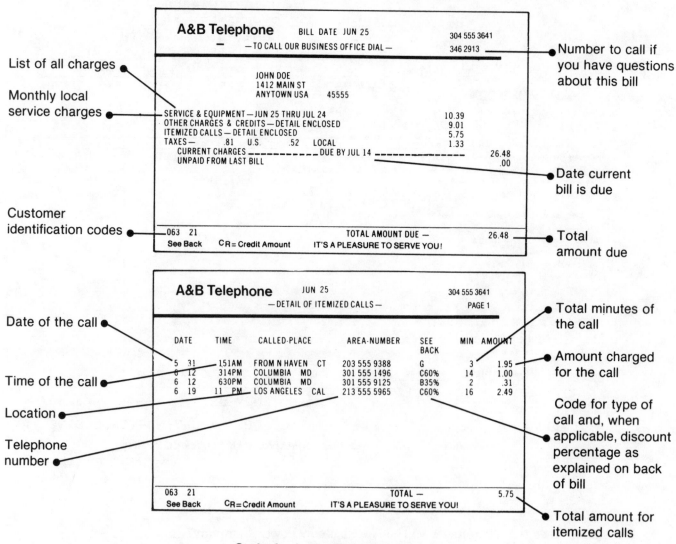

List of all charges

Monthly local service charges

Customer identification codes

A&B Telephone BILL DATE JUN 25   304 555 3641
— TO CALL OUR BUSINESS OFFICE DIAL —   346 2913

JOHN DOE
1412 MAIN ST
ANYTOWN USA   45555

SERVICE & EQUIPMENT — JUN 25 THRU JUL 24	10.39
OTHER CHARGES & CREDITS — DETAIL ENCLOSED	9.01
ITEMIZED CALLS — DETAIL ENCLOSED	5.75
TAXES — .81 U.S. .52 LOCAL	1.33
CURRENT CHARGES ———— DUE BY JUL 14 ————	26.48
UNPAID FROM LAST BILL	.00

063 21
See Back   CR = Credit Amount   TOTAL AMOUNT DUE —   26.48
IT'S A PLEASURE TO SERVE YOU!

Number to call if you have questions about this bill

Date current bill is due

Total amount due

Date of the call

Time of the call

Location

Telephone number

A&B Telephone JUN 25   304 555 3641
— DETAIL OF ITEMIZED CALLS —   PAGE 1

DATE	TIME	CALLED-PLACE	AREA-NUMBER	SEE BACK	MIN	AMOUNT
5 31	151AM	FROM N HAVEN CT	203 555 9388	G	3	1.95
6 12	314PM	COLUMBIA MD	301 555 1496	C60%	14	1.00
6 12	630PM	COLUMBIA MD	301 555 9125	B35%	2	.31
6 19	11 PM	LOS ANGELES CAL	213 555 5965	C60%	16	2.49

063 21
See Back   CR = Credit Amount   TOTAL —   5.75
IT'S A PLEASURE TO SERVE YOU!

Total minutes of the call

Amount charged for the call

Code for type of call and, when applicable, discount percentage as explained on back of bill

Total amount for itemized calls

Code for Long Distance Rates

G - Operator Assisted
C - Nights/Weekends
B - Weekday Evenings

*Information shown on this sample bill is for illustration purposes only. Rates shown do not necessarily reflect those that apply to your service.

Activity 17

Interpreting your phone bill

The A&B Telephone Company sent its customers a sample phone bill like the one on p. 56. The sample illustrates each part of a monthly bill. Use the sample bill to complete these statements.

About the total bill:

1. The customer's telephone number is _____ .

2. He has been billed for his service and equipment from June 25th through _____ .

3. The telephone number of the business office for the telephone company is _____ .

4. The date of this bill is _____ .

5. This bill should be paid by _____ .

6. The local service charge for one month is $ _____ .

7. The itemized long-distance calls come to $ _____ .

8. Federal and local taxes come to $ _____ .

9. The balance from the last bill is $ _____ .

10. The total amount the customer owes is $ _____ .

About the itemized long-distance calls:

1. On May 31st, the customer received a collect call from _____ , Connecticut.

2. The call was three minutes long and costs $ _____ .

3. The Connecticut telephone number is _____ .

4. On June 12th two calls were made to _____ , Maryland.

5. The two calls total _____ minutes of conversation.

Dial-direct interstate rates: making out-of-state calls

When you make long-distance calls to other states, the telephone company charges you interstate rates. You may dial these calls without the operator. If you do, you get Dial-Direct Interstate rates. Rates vary depending on the time and day of the week. Calls placed at night or on weekends are the least expensive.

CHECK YOUR UNDERSTANDING OF UTILITY BILLS

Below is a chart showing the times when various direct-dial long distance telephone rates are in effect. Study the chart then answer questions 1-5.

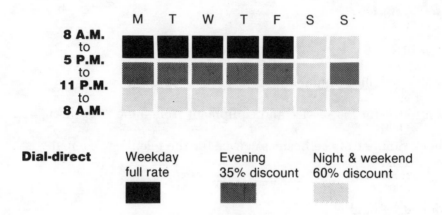

Dial-direct

| Weekday full rate | Evening 35% discount | Night & weekend 60% discount |

1. These rates apply to calls made without the services of the _____ .

2. When you dial direct on weekdays from 8 A.M. to 5 P.M., you pay the _____ rate.

3. When you dial direct from 8 A.M. to 5 P.M. on Saturday or Sunday, you get a _____ discount off the full rate.

4. When you dial direct on weekday evenings from 5 P.M. to 11 P.M., you get a _____ discount off the full rate.

5. The Nights/Weekends rate applies any day of the week, as long as the call is made between _____ P.M. and _____ A.M.

Decide whether the following statements are TRUE (T) or FALSE (F).

_____ **6.** Utility companies know how much you have used their service by reading the meter at your house or apartment building.

_____ **7.** A disconnect notice means that the utility company will turn off your service if you do not pay your bill within a certain period of time.

_____ **8.** Most utility companies bill their customers every month.

_____ **9.** The best rates for a direct-dial long distance call are on Sunday evenings after 5 p.m.

_____ **10.** A kilowatt hour refers to units of natural gas.

ANSWER KEY

USING DIRECTORIES

Activity 1, p. 2
1. 3 **2.** 1 **3.** 2 **4.** 2 **5.** 2 **6.** 2 **7.** 1 **8.** 1 **9.** 2 **10.** 3
11. 2 **12.** 3 **13.** 2 **14.** 2 **15.** 1 **16.** 1 **17.** 1 **18.** 2
19. 3 **20.** 3 **21.** 1 **22.** 3 **23.** 2 **24.** 1 **25.** 1 (or 3)
26. 2 **27.** 1 **28.** 1 **29.** 2 **30.** 1

Activity 2, p. 3
1. seventh **2.** fifth **3.** seventh if you are female; third or seventh if you are male **4.** third **5.** fourth **6.** fifth **7.** sixth
8. fourth **9.** seventh **10.** seventh

Activity 3, p. 4
1. 10; 10 **2.** 10 **3.** no **4.** yes **5.** 10 **6.** yes **7.** Martin Wholesalers **8.** Marvel Photos **9.** one **10.** one **11.** 6 or 7
12. Dr. Harry Boston, 708; Sibeski Brothers, 502; Dr. Harold Claytor, 611; Dr. David Daniels, 613; Dr. Paul Morrison, 707; Dr. Pauline Zee, 605; World Enterprises, 1013; Tami Studios, 510

Activity 4, p. 6
1. Periodicals—Current and Microfilm; Newspapers **2.** three
3. General Reference and Science **4.** two **5.** General Reference (behind Readers' Adviser's desk) **6.** yes

Check Your Understanding, p. 7
1. five **2.** Section A (A-5) **3.** Section D (D-5) **4.** Section A
5. Any two of the following: Dallas Kids; Eaton's Department Store; Kids' World; Walton's Department Store

Activity 5, p. 9
1. 555-8332 **2.** 555-4149 **3.** 555-8866 **4.** 555-3321
5. 555-7899 **6.** 555-8254

Activity 6, p. 9
1. 555-2813 **2.** 555-3245 **3.** 555-6471 **4.** three **5.** 555-7110
6. 555-3331

Activity 7, p. 10
1. Answers will vary but may include: easy to locate all businesses offering the service, product, or specialty you are looking for; easy to find store that is most conveniently located; may be able to find out hours; may be able to get directions; may be able to call ahead and check if item is available. **2.** yellow pages **3.** white pages (Since you already know the name of the shop, the white pages should be faster.)

Activity 8, p. 11
Furniture Listings
1. c **2.** c **3.** a **4.** b **5.** b **6.** a (sometimes b) **7.** a **8.** b
9. c **10.** a

Car Businesses
1. d **2.** d **3.** b **4.** b **5.** d **6.** d **7.** a **8.** d **9.** d **10.** a
11. c **12.** e **13.** c **14.** a **15.** c **16.** c

Activity 9, p. 12
1. dry cleaners **2.** DeLuxe Dry Cleaners Plant **3.** Sudden Service Cleaners **4.** yes (heading says *Cleaners—Cont'd*) **5.** a service **6.** Phyl's One Hour Martinizing **7.** Mr. Suds Dry Cleaning; Querbach Leather Process Inc.; Suburban Dry Cleaners & Shirt Launderers **8.** Guida Dry Cleaners **9.** Realgood Cleaners

Activity 10, p. 13
1. a **2.** c **3.** c **4.** a **5.** c **6.** a **7.** c **8.** a **9.** a **10.** a
11. c **12.** c **13.** a **14.** c **15.** a **16.** c **17.** c **18.** c
19. c **20.** c

Activity 11, p. 13
1. South Carolina, 803; South Dakota, 605; Wyoming, 307; Utah, 801 **2.** Alaska, 907; Hawaii, 808; Bermuda, 809; Puerto Rico, 809
3. Ontario Canada, 807, 705, 519, 416, 613; Quebec, 819, 418, 514; Saskatchewan, 306 **4.** Florida—three (904, 305, 813); West Virginia—one (304); Georgia—two (404, 912); Montana—one (406); Texas—six (806, 817, 915, 214, 713, 512) **5.** San Antonio (512); Houston (713); Dallas (214) **6.** 215 **7.** 404

Activity 12, p. 15
Situation #1: A. Mr. Brown just left for lunch. New York time: 12:01 P.M.
Situation #2: C. Call back in an hour. Des Moines time: 2:00 P.M.

Check Your Understanding, p. 16
1. S **2.** Carpenters **3.** Automobile Repairing and Service; Foreign Car Repairs **4.** Look under Plumbing; Plumbers; or Plumbing & Heating. **5.** P **6.** 10:30 A.M. **7.** b **8.** MacDonald; Mack; Major; McKay; McNeil; Miner

SPECIAL READING SKILLS

Activity 1, p. 20
1. C **2.** A **3.** E **4.** H **5.** B **6.** F **7.** D **8.** G **9.** I **10.** J

Activity 2, p. 23
1. G **2.** D **3.** H **4.** F **5.** B **6.** I **7.** C **8.** A **9.** K **10.** E

Activity 3, p. 25
1st row: regulatory, regulatory, service and guide
2nd row: warning, warning, service and guide

Check Your Understanding, p. 26
1. No U turn
2. Curve ahead
3. Intersection—watch for cars crossing, entering, or leaving highway
4. Picnic table
5. No right turn
6. Watch for schoolchildren
7. No trucks
8. A bridge or underpass ahead; clearance is 12 feet, 6 inches
9. Hill—drivers must take special care
10. Traffic may be moving into your lane; be ready to change your speed or lane

Activity 4, p. 30
1. 3-I (or I-3) **2.** 2-H (or H-2) **3.** 6-I (or I-6) **4.** 2-E (or E-2)
5. 1-H (or H-1)

Activity 5, p. 31
1. 75,375 **2.** north/south **3.** Hall of Justice **4.** Wayne County Community College **5.** Take Larned Avenue west to Woodward Avenue. Take Woodward Avenue north to Temple. Take Temple west to Cass Park. **6.** Joe Louis Arena, Cobo Hall, Cobo Arena, Veterans' Memorial, Ford Auditorium, City-County Building (some students may add Renaissance Center) **7.** c. southwest corner

Check Your Understanding, p. 33
1. 83, 70, 95, 395, 695, 895 **2.** 1, 40 **3.** I-95 **4.** 895 (Harbor Tunnel) or 695 (Francis Scott Key Bridge) **5.** Belair Road
6. yes **7.** I-695 **8.** Patapsco Valley State Park **9.** Take Route 1 north to Route 40. Take Route 40 east into Baltimore.

Activity 6, p. 37
1. eight **2.** 63, 69, 73, 71, 75, 65, 49, 79 **3.** 63 **4.** The Niagara Rainbow **5.** 8:40 A.M. **6.** 11:30 P.M. **7.** Albany-Rensselaer NY; Albany-Rensselaer, NY; Albany-Rensselaer, NY; Buffalo, NY

Activity 7, p. 38
1. Augusta, Ga.: 88/918; 4:25 P.M.; 6:25 P.M.; 1; Charleston, W. Va.: 60; 8:10 A.M.; 8:52 A.M.; 0; Columbia, S.C.: 88/918; 4:25 P.M.; 7:01 P.M.; 2
2. Atlanta, Ga.: 5; Chicago, Ill.: 3; Columbus, Ohio: 1
3. 943
4. yes
5. Atlanta
6. 951
7. Atlanta, Charleston (W. Va.); Fayetteville/Fort Bragg, Greenville/Spartanburg (S.C.); Hickory/Lenoir/Morganton (N.C.); Knoxville/Oak Ridge (Tenn.); (any four)
8. Saturdays

Activity 8, p. 40
1. 3:10; yes 2. 3:00; no 3. Flight #49; Flight #74; Flight #39
4. no; the plane is landing 5. 4:15; no 6. no 7. yes; 33
8. Flight #412 9. Detroit

Activity 9, p. 41
1. Philadelphia and Ocean City 2. down 3. up 4. 10:05
5. 6:05; 6:35 6. 6:50; 8:25; 8:40 7. State Road, DE 8. 1st STOP: Salisbury, MD; 2nd STOP: Bethany Beach, DE; 3rd STOP: Rohoboth Beach; 4th STOP: Lewes; 5th STOP: Milford; 6th STOP: Harrington; 7th STOP: Dover; 8th STOP: Smyrna; 9th STOP: State Road, DE (New York passengers connect at the State Road stop to go from Philadelphia to Ocean City and Ocean City to Philadelphia. Since New York is not between Ocean City and Philadelphia, it *is not* listed after State Road, DE.); 10th STOP: Wilmington, DE; 11th STOP: Chester, PA; 12th STOP: Philadelphia, PA 9. 6:50
10. 6:50

Check Your Understanding, p. 43
Down: 1. The Pioneer 2. 25; 26 3. 11:25 P 4. 12:20 A
5. 12:35 A 6. 11:10 A; 1:30 P; 6:00 P; 6:21 P 7. 9:50 P
Up: 1. 7:10 A 2. Tacoma, WA 3. 11:00 A 4. 11:00 A
5. Ontario, OR; Nampa, ID; Shoshone, ID 6. Ogden, UT
7. 7:10 A

Activity 10, p. 46
1. 54 2. 36 3. 93 4. December 5. August 6. Florence, South Carolina 7. Asheville, North Carolina 8. Savannah, Georgia

Activity 11, p. 48
1. accross 2. down 3. no 4. Beach Fork, Bluestone, Hawks Nest, Pricketts Fort, Tygart Lake 5. Blackwater Falls, Cacapon, Tygart Lake 6. the letter *N*

Activity 12, p. 49
1. the track team 2. the cheerleaders 3. 65 4. 68 5. the track team; the cheerleaders 6. the cheerleaders

Activity 13, p. 50
1. 300 2. 200 3. 31–35 4. 500 5. 31–35 6. 17–20 and 26–30 age groups 7. 500 8. females

Activity 14, p. 51
1. c 2. a 3. d 4. b 5. d

Check Your Understanding, p. 52
1. 1.6 (or 1.60935) 2. use the same reading as miles to kilometers (Locate the MPH by reading down and across. The point where the two meet gives the km/h.) 3. 88.5 4. 321.9 5. 8.0 6. 112.7
7. 56.3 8. 67.6 9. multiply the number of miles by 0.6 10. 6.25

Activity 15, p. 54
1. 783 2. 788 3. five 4. $15.39 5. penalty (late) 6. $1.00
7. 327-7161 8. 325-9164 9. fuel adjustment 10. no

Activity 16, p. 55
1. $75.30 2. $49.56 3. 562 4. every month 5. $1.05
6. $0.50 7. November 3 8. residential 9. $49.56
10. 2-011-11-10824-0-5

Activity 17, p. 57
About the total bill: 1. 304-355-3641 2. July 24th
3. 346-2913 4. June 25th 5. July 14th 6. $10.39 7. $5.75
8. $1.33 9. 0 10. $26.48

About the itemized long-distance calls: 1. N. Haven 2. $1.95
3. 203-555-9388 4. Columbia 5. 16

Check Your Understanding, p. 58
1. operator 2. full 3. 60% 4. 35% 5. 11 P.M., 8 A.M. 6. T
7. T 8. T 9. F 10. F